A GRAIN of WHEAT

Giving Voice to the Spirit of Change

Dr. Chuck Lofy

Edited by Gail Steel

Very truly, I tell you, unless a grain of wheat falls into the earth and dies, it remains just a single grain; but if it dies, it bears much fruit.

(John 12:24)

For Mary

A Grain of Wheat
by Dr. Chuck Lofy

Introduction

This is not a book I wrote or ever would have written. Rather, it is a book I spoke. At Gail Steel's insistent urging, I allowed her to have my words transcribed and to recast them in manuscript form. We are both aware of the shortcomings of such an endeavor, but I have to trust her sense that even in its present form, the ideas here presented will be helpful to some.

A Grain of Wheat is intended primarily for pastors and other church leaders, ordained and lay alike, but my hope is that the message will reach beyond the church. There is a great hunger these days for meaningful, relevant spirituality, and many are looking both inside and outside the church for spiritual feeding. It is offered as a gift to those wanting something beyond their agenda, something beyond the challenge or the task, the achievement, beyond the need to belong or to win. It is intended for the wounded and the seeker, for people like myself.

My goal is to share as simply as I can what I have learned on my journeys into change. I want to apply that learning to the changes currently underway in mainline denominations of the church, but you most likely will find applications for other areas of your lives. I encourage you to go wherever you might be led, and to stop, as Ignatius Loyola once suggested, where you find fruit.

The purpose of this book then is not merely to state a theory of change, but to stimulate the practice of changing. If it helps you to understand change better, that's good. But if it helps you to traverse the chaos and despair of change, if it shines light on the rebirth that inevitably follows death, we will both experience a reward beyond expectation.

Chuck Lofy

Forward

Chuck Lofy left professional service to the church many years ago, but his interest in organized religion and spiritual matters in general has never waned. Until recently his involvement with churches or religious organizations had seldom been business related. Chuck is now a change consultant to businesses, schools, *and churches.*

I first invited him to speak at the *Changing Church for a Changing World* conference in October, 1991, and our paths have crossed often since then. He has been welcomed back five more times and also joined us at several regional conferences. His passion translates into a powerful message for these turbulent times, which raises the life and teachings of Jesus Christ to a new relevance. His popularity is earned and understandable. *We would be remiss not to hear him with an enlightened sense of urgency.*

A Grain of Wheat is the summation of his messages at the Changing Church conferences. By becoming immersed in the material, as well as having experienced the presentations when they were delivered and felt their impact on the audiences, I was compelled to bring the message to you in some written form. Understand that sometimes quotation marks are loosely used in order to better tell a story. You may also notice repitition in a couple places. I am both aware of and responsible for the weaknesses resulting from this procedure, but I remain convinced that in this case, the end justifies the means.

There will be more forthcoming, much more I expect. Meanwhile, we have these pearls from which to claim our voice.

Gail Steel, Editor

Part I

Understanding Change

"Deep within us all there is an amazing inner sanctuary of the soul, a holy place, a Divine Center, a speaking Voice, to which we may continuously return. Eternity is at our hearts, pressing upon our time-torn lives, warming us with intimations of an astounding destiny, calling us home unto itself. Yielding to these persuasions, gladly committing ourselves in body and soul, utterly and completely, to the Light Within, is the beginning of true life."

Thomas Kelly

Chapter 1

The Heroic Journey

In 1922 T.S. Eliott's brilliant poem, "The Wasteland," prophesied that America was basically moving into a wasteland of rock and no water. *(Harcourt Brace & Co., 1932)*

In a dismal series of broken images, one can almost feel the scorching heat of the unblocked sun. The life-giving solar energy that fuels a balanced world becomes an instrument of death in a barren desert. Without the refreshing, thirst-quenching, life-giving splash of wet and cool, shade is denied, and roots and branches are withered. Life is reduced to "fear in a handful of dust."

And so the rock, the dry stone without the splash, the refreshment of water, is really our agenda. It is what Jesus called, "the flesh," the reality of control without soul. In our day to day lives, as you well know, the agenda often crystallizes and becomes concrete. After a while, the agenda has us, rather than we having control of the agenda. This happens in our personal lives. It happens in our marriages; it happens in our families; it happens in our churches and in our places of work.

Renewal is initiated when we begin to experience discomfort at being enslaved to the agenda, and we have the courage to momentarily leave, to separate from it. It's a courageous act, which is why it is called "the heroic journey," to honor a Sabbath, to separate from the form or the task to a place of rest, in order to experience a transformation of soul. It is in that time of vacation, which is derived from the Latin word "vacare," meaning "to empty," in that period of emptiness, that we touch our inner resources, the inner wellsprings that give life meaning and direction.

The goal is to come away renewed . . . recreated . . . regenerated . . . with a new sense of vision, passion and purpose. By wrestling with the journey throughout its course, taking the opportunity to reflect, to dream, to share with someone, to sleep on the pieces that are not easily digested, we will in truth be empowered. We can be assured of hope in our new perspective and power because it is as old as time itself, archetypal, universal, and eternally alive in the human heart.

From the Beginning of Time

You may be familiar with a television series from a few years ago called *Twin Peaks.* When it first aired, a commentary appeared on the editorial page of the *Minneapolis Star and Tribune* entitled, "The Twin Peak's Quest," carrying the subtitle, "Themes as Old as Homer Translated for TV." The author referred to the character of FBI agent Dale Cooper as a hero on a quest and compared him to other heroes throughout literature. He described the experience of watching the show "rewarding," as rewarding in fact as reading Homer's *The Odyssey,* Bernard Malamud's *The Natural,* or Larry McMurtry's *Lonesome Dove.* He pointed out that it is essentially the same timeless journey being chronicled, with only a change in the hero's hair style or clothing.

The article went on to outline the three elements in the

journey—the separation from the old pattern—the road of trials, suffering, and even failure, until finally there is some sort of new perspective gained—and then the return. In the end, the commentator declared, *what's ultimately important is the journey itself.*

> The journey is actually rooted in the very bottom of the collective unconscious we carry in us, and it resides there only to bubble to the surface in various ways.

It is reported that when Stephen Spielberg, the Jewish filmmaker of the movie *E.T.,* understood he had produced a story of resurrection, he was astonished. The metaphor of the heroic journey through death to new life is archetypal. It's rooted in the collective unconscious we carry in us, and it resides there only to bubble to the surface in various ways. It surfaces in authors writing manuscripts about the journey without even realizing they're part of a whole historic chain of similar stories.

The bottom line is simply this: it doesn't matter whether the person who writes it is conscious of its universality or not. Nor does it matter whether we in the audience consciously recognize the elements of the theme or not. We are moved to tears, laughter, awe, anger and resolve by how the hero, our surrogate, handles them. We recognize them in our bones as a metaphor of the journey each of us makes through this world from cradle to grave.

Confrontation with Death

The oldest piece of known written literature is the Babylonian epic of Gilgamesh, thought to be 5,000 years old. It is the story of a man whose very dear friend died. Gilgamesh, in his grief, was changed. He was so bereaved by the loss of his friend that he decided to search the world for a potion which would revive his friend. Thus he felt the call to adventure and went off to find the potion of immortality.

> Immortality is achieved not by holding
> on to what one has,
> but precisely by letting it go.

In the beginning he overcame terrific obstacles. He was forced to cross mountains and oceans, but all the way along he was provided with help. Guides appeared to him at various points to apprise him of the next step, until finally he was told by a wise old man and woman that he must go across the sea of death. *We must be confronted by, and we must confront, death. The only way change can occur is through the death of the old,* and that is why change is so scary.

So Gilgamesh traveled across the sea of death. Once on the other side, he was told that the potion for which he searched was, in fact, under the sea. Not a quitter, he journeyed beneath the sea and brought the potion back. He finally had it safely in his possession and set it down next to him while he rested, only to have a snake come by and eat it. All of his work seemed to be for naught, until finally Gilgamesh in his despair began to reflect on the snake. He came to see the snake as a symbol, a metaphor for life everlasting. It is, and always has been the metaphor for successful change because it can shed the old skin, develop new skin, and go on.

What Gilgamesh finally understood was that immortality is not holding on to the old; it's not holding on to his friend; it's precisely the opposite. It means letting his friend go, the way the snake lets go of his old skin. In that enlightenment, Gilgamesh was able to grieve. By surrendering to the death of his friend, he was forever changed. He now understood that life, indeed, is immortal. *Immortality is achieved not by holding on to what one has, but precisely by letting it go.*

Homer's great epics of the Greek era are much the same. *The Iliad* is the journey outward to the battles of Troy, and *The Odyssey* is the story of Odysseus returning home. During his journey he not only endured travails, but everything was taken from him. His boat was shipwrecked; all of his men were destroyed and he was left alone.

In his encounter with the Cyclops, the great one-eyed monster who imprisoned him and whom he finally blinded, his only means of escape was humility. He had to become *ou deis*. As Odysseus approached the gate, Polythemus asked, "Who are you?" He answered, "I am ou deis Odysseus," *ou deis* meaning *nobody* in Greek. Then the Cyclops responded, "If you're nobody, you may pass." Does that not express the essence of Christianity? When he finally became humble; when he finally gave up all the pretense; when he finally bent his knees ... "be merciful to me, oh Lord, a sinner" ... then finally he could be free of the one-eyed monster of the flesh. *He could be free of his ego.* He could then return to his true home.

In the Civil War Series on public television some time ago, Ken Burns at the outset referred to the Civil War as our epic, our *Iliad* and our *Odyssey*. It was the journey of a nation into conflict and into massacre, into carnage, until finally, out of that epic journey came a whole new vision for the future in the Emancipation Proclamation, "a new birth of freedom."

We see this theme in Dante's *Inferno* as well, where Dante, striving to get to paradise, understood his only chance was to first descend through purgatory, and finally down into the inferno for purification. Only then could he ascend into paradise.

We see it again in the wonderful Cervantes story, *Don Quixote*. This is a magnificent story of a man who is seen by everyone as crazy, when he wanders off in search of his impossible dream. To follow that impossible dream, to chase windmills only to be defeated at every turn, proved him not only crazy, but also stupid in everyone's eyes. Finally through his journey, he found redemption inside his own soul. He understood, as Joseph Campbell stated, "where we had thought to travel outward, we shall come to the center of our own existence."

(Princeton University Press 1968)

A Transformation of the Soul

My favorite film is the story of *Zorba the Greek*. It is the story of an Englishman, an intellectual with whom I closely identify. In the first scene of that film, the man is called to adventure. He has inherited from his father a mine off in a foreign country. Now, of course, this is an obvious metaphor of the mine of his own soul that needs exploring. It too is located in a far-off land. One must go down into the dark inner recesses of one's own being in order to extract the treasure that brings enrichment. Since he has no idea how to proceed, he hires a Greek named Zorba as his guide.

At one point Zorba admonishes him, "You think too much. What good are your books? If they don't explain death, what good do they do?"

You see, the Englishman is too much in his head, and somehow his journey is to find his way down inside of himself to his heart, and to his bones, and to his soul. "What will all this knowledge get you?"

The wonderful drama unfolds: Zorba the guide continues to teach, and the Englishman continues to resist his teaching, until finally, very slowly, the man begins to relent. He begins to *experience himself* and to adjust his ideas or his truths accordingly.

Experience leads him to fall in love with a widow from the town, and eventually he makes love with her. Unfortunately a local young man who has been infatuated with the woman, witnesses the affair, and in his despair, drowns himself. The town's people are so upset that they stone the woman and she tragically dies. The work in the mine fails as well. All is desolation and total devastation.

But in this process, the Englishman has learned something about Zorba. When Zorba is in pain, he dances. He dances himself into a frenzy until he finally collapses in exhaustion. In the final scene, the Englishman and Zorba are sitting on the beach waiting for the ship to return him to England. All is in ruin. The woman is dead, the mine has failed, the venture has ended in total defeat. It is then that the Englishman turns to Zorba and says, "Teach me to dance."

Zorba answers, "Dance? Did you say 'dance'? Come on, my boy!" The film ends with the two men dancing on the beach.

This is a story of transformation, the transformation of the Englishman's personality. The adventure started as a journey outward to work a mine and to make money, but it ended with the transformation of his own psyche... the heroic journey.

Dorothy takes the same heroic journey in the classic movie, *The Wizard of Oz*. She was living a colorless life in gray Kansas. Her life had no color. It had lost its dance and its music. She was blown by a tornado into this strange land of Oz. In the chaos of change, she found supernatural help from good witches and from the scarecrow, the tin man, and the lion, all of whom represent parts of herself. The tin man's need for a heart, the lion's desire for courage, and the scarecrow's wish for brains were all pieces of the transformational metaphor about to take place inside of Dorothy herself.

Her first destination was the Emerald City for an audience with the great wizard, the omniscient guide. But finding him wasn't enough. He sent her back out on a fearful, threatening but critical mission, to slay the dreaded witch of the West. By slaying the adversary and all the evil she represented, Dorothy was really slaying the evil within herself. She completed her mission only to discover when she returned that the great wizard was a very ordinary person on whom she had projected her own strength. Having experienced the Emerald City and the adventures of the journey, Dorothy would return to Kansas forever changed. And Kansas was no longer gray. Kansas was bathed in living color.

Rooted in Scripture

I believe the journey, which is played out over and over in literature, and in fairy tales and songs and epics all through history, finds its culmination in religion. The greatest stories in all religion involve a journey. Buddha took his long journey through his road of trials until he sat under the bao tree, an analog of the cross. There sitting under the bao tree, he withstood the temptations of war and false love and found enlightenment.

Moses heard the call to adventure in the Book of Exodus and began the classic hero's journey when he led the people out of Egypt into the chaos and confusion of the desert. In the beginning he resisted the role God assigned him. He stuttered; he wasn't a leader. He simply didn't want to do it. But the time had come for freedom, for slavery to become a thing of the past.

Someone had to speak, and someone had to lead the people.

Moses encountered great resistance from the guardians of the gate, the pharaohs who wanted to keep him and his people enslaved. But through the appearance of divine aid, he was able to cross through the Red Sea and to go out into the emptiness of the desert. There in the desert, the laws of the past no longer pertained. Just as the laws governing children, imposed from the outside, are not appropriate for adolescents and adults, so the laws which had controlled the Israelites in Egypt were outgrown. Chaos ruled. Finally Moses ascended the mountain and, in classic illumination and divine revelation, he understood that if they continued to destroy themselves, they would never survive as a people.

He descended from the mountain with the Ten Commandments, which set forth basic systems for then and for now, declaring, among other things, that they could not indiscriminately worship any and all gods. They could not indiscriminately cheat and lie to one another. They could not harm each other, or take one another's possessions or one another's spouses. They were being directed to mature as a people. They were expected to become internally responsible. We too must have internal laws, imposed not by an outside force, but implanted by the God of love and decency, if we are to survive as a people.

The journey is all there. The separation from Egypt was repeated by Moses' separation from his people and his ascent of Mount Sinai. The ignorant people considered him foolish. Moses was forced to destroy the Commandments because the people at first didn't understand. This is so often the way of the return, or the process of return, until an integration occurs between the new vision and the leftover life of the people. The Ten Commandments stand as one of the greatest boons of all time, one of God's greatest gifts to humanity.

In our time, my favorite example of the heroic journey is

that of Martin Luther King Jr. A Baptist minister in Montgomery, Alabama, and the son of a Baptist minister, King was called to destiny through the work of Rosa Parks. Parks and a group of women in Montgomery had long been training themselves for a boycott, until one day sheer exhaustion drove Rosa Parks to call her people to adventure. She refused to move to the back of the bus.

> ...the true guide always articulates
> what is in the heart of the people.

Out of that call a guide emerged, as had happened through the ages, a guide who articulated the vision of the people. We can be assured of the guide's integrity because *the true guide always articulates what is in the heart of the people.*

King arose to speak for the people. He embarked down his road of travails. From the earliest days of the movement toward integration, he encountered extraordinary resistence. A bomb was placed on the front porch of King's home, but still he did not question going forward. Eventually the trials began to involve more and more of his personal life.

After the birth of his first daughter, telephone calls came late at night threatening his daughter. In the Pulitzer Prize winning book by David Garrow, *Bearing the Cross (Morrow and Co., 1986),* the story is told of King becoming so devastated and disoriented by these threats to the life of his daughter that he sunk into deep despair. Around midnight, frantic, without direction, and unable to sleep, he sat alone at the kitchen table. He discovered in that moment that religion had to become real to him. He had to discover God for himself.

And King said, as he bowed over his kitchen table, he prayed out loud for courage. At that moment, Garrow recounts, King heard a voice with perfect clarity telling him to remain firm.

The voice he knew to be Jesus assured him that he would never be left alone. "He promised never to leave me, never to leave me alone. No never alone. No never alone. He promised never to leave me, never to leave me alone."

King stood up from that experience and never again doubted. He knew early on that he would be martyred. It was a foregone conclusion for him. He lived constantly in the acceptance that someday he would be killed. Every time the darkness hit, every time the questions intruded into his soul, he went back to that experience at the kitchen table, the experience called in literature, "the initiation."

"One knows deep down within," King wrote, "there is something in the very structure of the cosmos that will ultimately bring about fulfillment and the triumph of that which is right. And this is the only thing that can keep one going in difficult periods."

On the road of trials, one finds a strength from who knows where. It is derived from a source stronger than any ego or intelligence or emotion we now possess. It simply comes from a different realm.

The Quaker, Thomas Kelly, once wrote,

"Deep within us all there is an amazing inner sanctuary of the soul, a holy place, a Divine Center, a speaking Voice, to which we may continuously return. Eternity is at our hearts, pressing upon our time-torn lives, warming us with intimations of an astounding destiny, calling us home unto itself. Yielding to these persuasions, gladly committing ourselves in body and soul, utterly and completely, to the Light Within, is the beginning of true life."

The point of the journey is to touch that inner light, or, rather, to be touched by it because the human psyche left alone cannot draw that light to itself. It can only ask.

Jesus Christ: The Hero Within Us All

A holy old man in Rome taught me a law of the spiritual life: First of all we are led to the realization that we need something, and that knowledge alone, *to know that we have need,* is grace. Next we are given the grace to ask for what we need, and then, and only then, do we get it.

The hero in this spiritual journey is not the hero we normally picture, the football hero or the physical giant. In fact, in literature and religion the hero almost inevitably "loses," just as Christ "lost." The journey is always to the surrender of the ego, to the surrender of human power, in order to allow divine power to fill the void. It is heroic because we must first give up confidence in ourselves, in order to place power *outside of our control.* A person embarks on a hero's journey in search of help, just as the alcoholic who hit bottom has come to the realization of his or her own need. One is then brought to the point of "seek and you will find," "knock and it shall be opened to you," "ask, and you shall receive." *The paradox is that heroic stance of core humility.*

Protestants easily understand this attitude because it involves the traditional dispute between good works and faith, that core position of kneeling in the void before the divinity and simply saying, "Be merciful to me, I'm a sinner. You are going to have to love me first before I can perform." Such is the paradoxical stance of the hero, naked, helpless, in need of love and in need of grace.

The universal story of the heroic journey appears in all nations, all through time, and in all literature. One has to ask then, from where does it come? Carl Jung believes it is locked in our psychic system, just as the desire to eat is locked into our system, just as the need to procreate is locked into our system. He called it "archetypal," typed into the very fiber of our being.

(Princeton University, 1956)

Jesus, when he first received his call, was summoned out into the desert, where he began his road of trials, including his temptations. He encountered resistence at every turn. In his understanding of himself and his consciousness of his own divinity, he was tempted to exploit his miraculous powers — Satan:"If you are the Son of God, throw yourself down." The people:"Give us a sign." Thomas:"Far be it from you to suffer." Herod:"Work a miracle." The high priests:"Come down from the cross and we will believe." These temptations struck at the very core of Jesus' understanding of his divine self. He resisted those temptations to the end.

> Jesus lived his life, then separated from life
> by dying, and descended into hell.
> He returned in a new form with an entirely
> different vision...In his compassion
> he sent his Spirit to help us
> understand that mystery.

The prototype for all heroic journeys is the life, death, descent into hell, and resurrection of Jesus. In this paschal mystery he reenacted all that is universal in the human psyche. Jesus lived his life, then separated from life by dying, and descended into hell. He returned in a new form with an entirely different vision, a whole new knowledge of life and death. In his compassion he sent his Spirit to help us understand that mystery. "When the Spirit of truth comes, he will guide you into all the truth;..." (John 16:13)

Jesus' journey into the abyss is the prototype, the fulfillment of the archetypal drive embedded in the consciousness of humanity. He promised us that on the cross he would draw all things to himself. He would be the culmination of the reality that life always proceeds through suffering and death, and that beyond death is always new life. Life is not given to us to simply hold on to in a lateral way. Life is really a series of descents into hell and resurrections to new levels of conscious awareness.

Life, in my experience, is a spiral through which we grow to a certain point before experiencing some type of suffering or call. A separation is required from life as it has been, and during this transition time we must dig deeper into ourselves, in order to rise to a higher level of maturity. We are forced to unearth new sources of strength at each level, and, as the next testing stage presents itself, we must reach down even deeper. Finally, through this spiral of struggles, we have the capacity both to suffer more authentically than we ever have before and also to *fully* enjoy life.

Some years ago on his television program, singer Glen Campbell asked blues singer and pianist, Ray Charles, "Ray, what is soul?"

Charles answered, "Soul is the capacity to laugh deeply and to cry deeply and to know the difference." Soul is found at the end of life's spirals, after repeated cycles of death and rebirth.

• • •

Jesus' message was a call to shed old wineskins and put on new life, to express truth in a new wrap. Truth is the supreme goal, and if we are living a partial truth and become slaves to the lie, we will most certainly be called to adventure. We will be called out of the lie, out of the stagnation, out of the crystallization of form, into new life. The flesh, which I believe Jesus meant as the form, the structure or law, profits nothing alone. It is the spirit that gives life. The heroic journey is a return to the spirit.

The adventure always leads us
from one form to another,
through an intervening period of chaos,
disorientation and labor.
In the chaos,
one must dig down deep within oneself
in order to rise to a higher level.

As yet another form is outgrown,
one must reach down even deeper
before emerging once again
at a new and higher level.

Soul is found at the end of life's spirals,
after repeated cycles
of death and rebirth.

Chapter 2

A Passion For Form

Some time ago we received notice that our office answering service procedures would be changing, as they were adding some new features *for our benefit*. We were invited to attend a training session, but neither my wife nor I could be there. A few days later when I checked the answering service, it was programmed differently, and I couldn't gain access. I called for an explanation, and a gracious woman tried to instruct me.

I'm much more in my head, as you can imagine, and I just wasn't getting her explanation. I told her as much, so she put her supervisor on the phone. He continued with more foreign jargon, and I became even more confused, angry, and a little afraid of how all this was going to work for me. Finally, I said, "Look, I'm a consultant on change, and you're changing the rules. Everything I say in my workshops is happening to me—I'm angry, confused, upset and so on." At that point he became very gentle, and patiently invited me to come in and talk about it personally.

Even though I know the theory of change backward and forward, getting caught by it is unavoidable.

Change is a movement from one way of thinking or doing business to another, and it kicks up strong reactions. What happens to all of us is that we give ourselves to the forms in life. Rollo May, in his book *The Courage to Create, (Norton, 1975)* said that human beings have a passion for form. This is one of the most helpful things I've ever learned: we all need structure and organization. My mother used to begin every Saturday morning saying, "Let's get organized!"

This passion for form shows itself everywhere. People want

to know what the road map is, because form provides security, a haven that prevents a person from having to deal with all of reality at once. And the form provides efficiency, and efficiency gives identity. If I know what the rules are, I can predict what is expected of me. I can practice becoming efficient, and as I become more efficient, my identity is actually changed. I can say, "Hey, I'm a basketball player!" I have taken the discipline of the form. I've practiced it, become proficient at it, and now *become* it in a certain way.

Ministry is one example of form. A person goes through a certain curriculum, practices the skill, wears the clothes, graduates, and goes out into the world to practice this form. A pastor does not do certain things an engineer does and a radio announcer does not attempt to minister professionally.

My children used to play football in the front yard. They wouldn't decide the rules beforehand, and inevitably one of them would come in crying because he thought the goal line was the driveway. When he reached the driveway, the others said it was the tree on the far side of the driveway. In the newspaper comic strip "Calvin and Hobbes," the characters always make up the rules as they go. They seem to "thrive on chaos," to use Tom Peters' quote. In athletics it doesn't make any difference if the football field is 100 yards or 110 yards, as it is in Canada. The point is, you must decide ahead of time. A player can shoot across a basketball court and make the basket, but if the gun sounds before the shot is taken, the game is over. The basket doesn't count. That's the way it is because we have this passion for form. We always organize ourselves.

All of this sports discussion is leading somewhere, as we begin to understand why it's so difficult to make a paradigm shift. We, meaning all human beings, have a passion for form. But I believe it holds true not only of all human beings. I believe it's metaphysical. I believe in the school of thought that says form is linked to the very definition of ontology as we know it. In time and space, being shows itself in form. Energy shows itself in matter. A class or a conference is an example. One needs an agenda, a syllabus, or a bulletin in order to know how to divide time. In theological terms, we need commandments; we need boundaries.

Joel Barker tells us in the video *Discovering the Future* that the first function of the paradigm is to set boundaries. Once the boundaries are set, one knows what the rules are and can therefore determine what constitutes success. When the forms go, we have chaos. Chaos always results from the breakdown of form.

Salvador Minuchin, who pioneered work in the psychology of family systems *(Harvard University Press, 1974)*, came to the realization that what separates functional families from dysfunctional families is the presence or absence of a clear sense of boundaries. A few years ago I visited a state hospital for adolescents and asked the psychiatrist to describe some common characteristics of the teenagers who resided there. He said, invariably, they come from families without boundaries. He said that these children push for boundaries in the home and when none are set, they push in the schools for boundaries. When none are set in the schools, they push the police until finally someone gives them some boundaries. We don't know who we are without boundaries.

Spirit needs form of some kind. Spirit left to itself is psychotic, not incarnate. It's diffuse. Spirit has to be present in form, so that when a form expresses and releases its spirit, we have an epiphany, a manifestation of the spirit through that form. It's what religion is about; it's what art is about. All life has a passion for form.

I have come to understand that we have different levels of attachment to form. The first level of attachment is investment,

31

which describes your attachment to this book. You are investing your time and energy for a certain period of time. When the book is finished, you move on.

But there are other forms in which we involve more of ourselves. For example, I signed a contract for more than casual involvement in this book. I also wear a wedding ring. I'm committed to the form of my marriage. It's not just that I'm in my marriage today, but I'm committed to be in it tomorrow and the next day. My loan at the bank for my house is a signed commitment that I will continue to make payments. The more of myself that I commit to the form, the more invested I am in that form.

A higher level of investment is an identification with the form. To demonstrate the difference between commitment and identification, consider as an example the movie *Moonstruck*. You may recall the father, who is having an affair, takes his lover to the opera. His wife, left alone, has dinner in a restaurant by herself. She invites a man, who is also dining alone, to join her. After dinner the man asks if he may walk her home, and she agrees. When they arrive at her house, he propositions her, and she declines without hesitation *because she is married*. Then she makes a very interesting observation: "I know who I am." That's identification. She is married and will not accept the proposition, not only because it violates a commitment. It violates her identity.

It is possible to be in a relationship in which one is committed, but not identified. ·I have seen over and again companies that don't initiate their employees into an identification with their business. Often they barely orient them. There isn't a rite of passage that initiates people into what it means to belong to this company. Universities and churches are very good in this area (sometimes to a fault) and have developed ageless traditions around a high level of identification. Yet someone may be in the church and not be identified with it. A person has gone through the motions of baptism or confirmation but hasn't really internalized the consciousness of what Christianity is about.

The great Boston Celtic basketball teams of the past put this idea into practice with their players. If a player didn't think as a Celtic, if he didn't play as a Celtic, or have a sense of what it means to be a champion, that player, no matter who he was, didn't last long as a Celtic. To play with the Celtics one needed somehow to be initiated into that identity.

Levels of Attachment or Investment:
- Investment
- Commitment
- Identification
- At-one-ment

The fourth and highest level of investment occurs when we are at one with the form. There are times when the farmer out in the field becomes so at one with the work, land, and air, that he or she is transparent with the form. He and the form are one. Teachers know that experience as well. There are times when an instructor and the class feel like one organism, and in the end, one will walk out of the class and say, "I can't believe I'm being paid for this." Pastors experience this when the liturgy is just right. The transparency is even more powerful because of the mystical qualities intrinsic in spiritual expression.

There are times when you're making love with your spouse and you feel like you are every lover, that what you're doing is universal and has been done throughout all history, and you are privileged to be one sacramental expression of it.

A friend described to me an experience of jogging in Whitewater State Park. He said, "As I was jogging, I knew that I could run forever. And as I ran, I became totally at one with the universe and thought to myself, now I can die. It's okay for me to die. My life had meaning in that one moment."

You've heard the expression, "in the twinkling of an eye." Suddenly in that one moment, at a beach watching a sunset, looking into the eyes of your child, whatever it is... suddenly life lifts itself to a new level, and you say, "Yes." All the questions dissolve.

The most wonderful and scary relationships I have are those with my spouse, children, and friends, in which we speak together "from our bones." My mother always knew things through her bones. What makes these relationships frightening is that those bones don't care a bit about ego; bones don't lie. That's where the spirit is, I believe. It's essentially why people get sick if they're not living a spiritual life. When we are listening to the tissue and nervous system of our bodies, and we come down into harmony with ourselves, and are finally in touch with ourselves, everything feels "yes."

The journey to speaking the truth from our bones is also a journey to the source of creativity. The best ideas we have first sound crazy because the creative force comes out of spirit. It's not linked to form. Therefore, when a new idea comes out of spirit, necessarily the old paradigm sees it as crazy or heretical. According to Joel Barker, paradigm shifts always begin at the edge.

The journey is a journey down into the safety of the bones. The best working relationships I've ever been part of, the most effective organizations with which I've been associated, subscribed to "speaking the truth from the bones." In one case it became the executive council's password. They would never complete a decision until they had first agreed "in their bones." Bones don't lie.

The point I'm trying to make is that when one has invested in a form or a paradigm, is wholly committed, identified with the paradigm and at one with it, *change then asks one to give it up*. The more of myself I have invested, the harder it's going to be for me to give it up. But if I am identified with the spirit, rather than its form, I can leave it behind and still carry the life-giving energy of it with me.

Some people are so attached to the form, they go further than giving themselves *to* the form; they give themselves *away* to the form. This phenomenon is called projection. They unconsciously project themselves onto the form. They somehow come to think they are the form.

What happens when someone has no spiritual life? If a person hasn't an adequate sense of personhood, or God's presence, or faith, he or she will naturally become over-identified with form. If someone is brought up in an environment lacking unconditional love, mercy, and forgiveness, that person will develop what Scott Peck calls *self-esteem without self-love*. Self-esteem is rooted in performance and as long as one performs, succeeds, excels, all is well. The fear is that if one ever fails or relaxes, there will be nothing there. A person will never be able to ask forgiveness, according to Peck, if he or she does not have self-love.

I happen to be working with a person who is very much that way, and she is about to lose her job because of it. She doesn't know how to separate from the unapproachable role of star performer, to come down into herself and acknowledge to her staff that she's made mistakes and is lost. The alcoholic who can't stop drinking is convinced that even if he comes down into himself and says, "I need help," there will be no help.

Jesus brought into the world the great paradigm shift of Christianity... mercy, forgiveness. If you live by the law, you will die by the law. Christianity allows us to come down into our vulnerability. "Be merciful to me, I'm a sinner." But unfortunately those people who do not have self-love, mercy, forgiveness, who at the core of their existence must excel, become over-identified with form. They give themselves away to form. Then, if the form with which they have over-identified is taken away, they react destructively.

Christianity allows us to come down into our vulnerability.

This is why they killed Jesus. Christ tried to separate the Pharisees from an over-identification with law. The paradigm was the law; they had success under the law. Jesus called them hypocrites, living in ego, living in self-satisfaction. They walked past the wounded and knew nothing about healing. They locked the doors to the kingdom of heaven and threw away the keys. "If you were blind, you would not be guilty of sin; but now that you claim you can see, your guilt remains."(John 9:41) There's something other than law, he said. There's love and there's mercy, woundedness, healing — and they killed him.

Resistance to change manifests itself in two ways: normal and abnormal. The normal resistance to change is related to the investment, commitment, identification, and the at-one-ment with form. An abnormal grip on the known is born in low self-esteem and in the failure to experience a spiritual life. Change is never a neutral experience. In fact, it kicks up incredibly strong reactions. The intensity of the feeling is directly proportionate to the level of involvement. The deeper the involvement, the more resistance.

Another element that often contributes to the intensity of resistance to change is timing. It has to do with whether or not the change is developmental or unexpected. For a parent to be taken from a young child is not developmentally anticipated, worse yet for a child to be taken from a parent. But when we have a chance to prepare for change, when we have a chance to anticipate retirement, a person dying, a child going off to college, what Gail Sheehy calls "predictable passages," we are able to ease into letting go. *(Dutton, 1976)* Stuart Alsop, who wrote *Stay of Execution*, a diary of his own experience as he was dying of leukemia, closed the book by saying, "Just as there is a time for tired, sleepy people to sleep, so there is a time for dying people to die."*(Lippincott, 1973)* In other words, there is a readiness, a fullness of time, a sense of completion.

The prophet smells the death of form.

Change is a separation from the form. Change separates spirit from form. The more of my spirit I have in that form, the more I am going to resist change. If I'm really hooked into the form, when adverse information comes my way, I won't even see or hear that information. I'll just manage to shut it out. If new information filters through and begins to pull me apart, I will become angry. I am connected to this, and someone or something is trying to separate me from it. The more force that accompanies the outside influence, the more resistant I become. My first reaction is denial; the second is anger. As new information comes in, I might try to negotiate, make concessions so as not to separate. And if the call to separation continues, I may even go into rage. I believe it's very important for leaders to understand that in asking for change, they may be evoking the demon of rage.

What distinguishes rage from anger? Anger is specific, focused. When I'm angry at someone, I'm angry for a specific reason. Rage is global, diffuse; rage has no target. Pastors see it all the time. People in grief are often enraged without a specific target, simply because it's a necessary part of the separation process. Is God the target? Is it a person? No, it's nonspecific. It's diffuse rage.

If, to further complicate things, that rage is experienced by someone who is over-identified with form, who doesn't possess a clear sense of self, and the security of form is removed, — *his* money, *her* beauty, *his* health is taken away — *somehow s/he is wholly displaced. Then* s/he may become violent. The underlying threat is loss of "self."

"My farm is gone, and all I know is farming. All I am is a farmer. I may now get the gun and start killing bankers, or myself, or whoever is in the way." People who are over-identified with the form will not only put up great resistance to change, they may even kill rather than change.

The prophet smells the death of the form. "But Jesus said to him, 'Follow me, and let the dead bury their own dead.'" *(Matthew 8:22)* When the prophet calls someone who does not have a strong spiritual core, there will always be over-determined resistance to change.

Chapter 3

The Dance Of Spirit

Spirituality involves being so centered in the spirit that one sees the dance of forms. The church today is not what it was fifty years ago. People who have spirit can dance about that. People who don't have a spiritual sense see it as a great catastrophe. You're getting older. Yes, can you dance? Your children are leaving home. Yes, can you dance? The forms are always shifting. It is the spirit that gives life!

People resist change for one reason: they're afraid.

Impressionist painters of the nineteenth century were vilified by the art establishment because their theory so contradicted the prevailing paradigms of art. The impressionists realized that all we see is light. Realizing that if we were to turn off all the lights, we wouldn't see each other, they reasoned that we don't see things; we only see light. Fascinated by that discovery, they decided to paint light. They painted light on clouds, light dancing on water. Instead of painting the substance of haystacks, Monet painted the beautiful colors radiating off the haystacks. Instead of painting the cathedral at Rouen, he painted the light the cathedral reflected. The French Academie challenged him and finally excommunicated him. Most of the impressionists went hungry because they separated from the paradigm.

People resist change for one reason: they're afraid. Fear and anxiety go together the way anger and rage go together. In fear, we are afraid of a very specific thing. Anxiety is diffuse; we don't know what it is we are afraid of. That's why anxiety is so terrifying.

In the process, as the new information continues to come in, when finally I realize I can no longer hold my emerging self in this form, there comes a critical moment of despair. That is the decisive turning point in change. Despair, I believe, is the most painful emotion there is. It is particularly painful for people who are trying to live a life of faith because they may think that faith is the antithesis of despair. It's not. Rollo May has said, "Joy is on the far side of despair." *(Norton, 1975) Faith is not the refusal to go into despair; faith is the willingness to go through despair. Faith is not a contradiction to despair, but rather it is what accompanies us in despair.* I know from experience that we practice hope far more when things seem hopeless. Only when things seem hopeless can faith come into play.

Faith is the willingness to go through despair.

It's there in despair that one feels

the movement of the spirit.

Scott Peck in *The Different Drum,* admits that before most groups with whom he's working can successfully achieve community, he must empty himself of controlling tendencies and be willing to fail. *(Simon and Schuster, 1987)* I know the feeling. Every time I'm satisfied with my work as a speaker or consultant, I have first experienced despair. I've sat silent in sessions when people have emptied themselves, and I've wondered, "What am I doing here?"

But it's only there in despair that one feels the movement of the spirit. *Only* there. We *must be willing to experience despair.*

Why do people resist despair? Because we have a passion for form. We want answers and a clear set of expectations for success. It's too painful and lonely in the darkness of despair. Joel Barker is right when he tells us the rules change with the paradigm shift. When the paradigm shifts, we're all back at zero, and who wants to start over?

I drove 350 miles from Mankato, Minnesota, to Milwaukee, Wisconsin, to attend a workshop of Scott Peck's, to thank him for the idea of emptiness. Peck, I believe, is a holy man, holy because of his practice of emptiness. Christians have to learn to live in emptiness. If we are afraid of our own despair, we will never heal the despair rampant in the world.

Transparent to the Transcendent

The ancient Greeks devoted much intellectual energy to questions like: What is the earth? What constitutes being? Earth, air, fire, water? Pythagorus said being is form and without form one cannot access being. The problem with God for many of us is that God is formless. God is beyond form. God is the source from whom all forms arise, but God is not a form. The only way to access God is through metaphors, through images, forms that point beyond themselves to that nameless mystery that is beyond form.

Religion is supposed to create forms that are transparent to God, transparent to the transcendent. Liturgies and worship services are meant to be epiphanies. Their forms are meant to simultaneously hide and reveal the divine. They are not divine, but they point to the divine. They're like stained glass windows in the cathedrals of Christendom that point beyond themselves. The window is useless without the sunlight shining through it.

What can happen is that people or organizations who are not in touch with the spirit can give themselves away to form through a phenomenon called projection. *The spirit, rather than being illuminated by the form, is lost in the form.*

The heresies of our time are primarily the result of "absolutizing" forms. One may not absolutize any form. You may not literalize any metaphor. I was brought up believing in the absolute nature of the Catholic church, and am now able to salute a very effective Vatican II for beginning to crack some of the walls of fear around the Catholic church. There is a new reformation taking place among Catholics.

The one thing we do know is that God is not a form. God is spirit and seeks those who will worship in spirit.

One of my favorite conversations in scripture is when Jesus and Nicodemus are talking about being born again. Nicodemus asks, "How can anyone be born after having grown old? Can one enter the second time into the mother's womb and be born?" (John 3:4)

At that point, I just have to believe Jesus looked at Nicodemus and smiled. In so many words he said, "You're a leader of Israel and you don't get it? I'm talking metaphor! I'm talking spirit, you're talking flesh."

Over and over Jesus talked in metaphor, in parable, in spirit. Over and over we don't get the metaphor. We crystallize the metaphor, unable to see through it to the divine. God the Father is a metaphor. The great mystics of all time have seen God in a multitude of metaphors. God is a garden; God is a diamond; God is a lover; God is a friend; God is a Divine Self. There are countless metaphors for God. Jesus most often referred to God as "Father," but when people crystallize around that "Father" form, some will go to war about whether or not God can be called a Mother.

How can I tell you God is not a Mother, if that's the way you've experienced God? If you tell me the experience I had on a mountain top was not real or Godly, how can I relate to you? Scott Peck says that God pursues us like a lover and that the passion for God is not at all unlike the love that a man and woman have for each other. If that's his experience of God, how can I take that away from him? Why would I have to take that away from him and say, "No, no, no, God isn't a lover." Why would I even want to? How do I know that God isn't a lover?

In our experience of the ineffable, *the one thing we do know is that God is not a form*. That we know. God is spirit and seeks those who will worship in spirit. If I don't have a spiritual life, I can't understand. I don't get it. So, I'll call you a heretic because I don't know what you're talking about in a metaphorical sense. I don't know God. *But for those who know God as spirit, the metaphor will never be in the way. It will lead us to a direct experience of God.*

Spirit and the Kingdom Within

Daryl Stingley played wide receiver for the Purdue Boilermakers football team and later went on to a professional career with the Boston Patriots. When he was twenty-four, he went out for a pass and received instead a blow to the back of his neck. Stingley instantly became a quadriplegic. A few years later when the Patriots were playing the Chicago Bears in the Superbowl, Stingley was interviewed about his experience. He talked about his travels around the country visiting rehabilitation centers and talking to others who had recently become physically impaired. His message to them urged them to become stronger in spirit, assuring them that strength of spirit is not so bad. He told them his spirit was stronger now than ever. He talked about being better off than his teammates because of what happened to him, because of having to grow spiritually and emotionally in a way that his teammates couldn't understand. He closed the interview with these incredible words: "Spiritually and emotionally, my cup runneth over."

Where does that spirit come from?

From where did it come, when a man I was counseling emerged from despair at his wife's abandonment, to ask if we could have a joint session with her? He was ready to thank her for walking out and finally bringing him to his senses.

From where did the spirit come that allowed a woman struck with a debilitating disease to give up her nursing career, get a masters degree and write her paper on the integration of body, mind, heart and spirit?

What is this power inside that transforms our thinking? "The spirit gives life. The flesh counts for nothing." *(John 6:63NIV)* The real power is in the spirit.

> The fundamental task of change is to lead
> people back to a spiritual existence,
> to an existence that is alive...

That power is seen in the woman who searched her house and finally found her precious gold coin. The real power is possessed by those who use change as an invitation to reclaim their gold coin. The alcoholic discovered that the only way to escape the claws of alcoholism was to reclaim the gold coin. It's the only way an unemployed executive, who for the first time found himself in a position of powerlessness, was somehow able to access the power of the Spirit. These people I have met down through the years have taught me again and again that it's *not what happens to us that is decisive, but rather how we deal with it*. They have taught me what was meant by the wise seer who once said, "The only way out is through." Such is the summation of all teaching about change. Creative change culminates in death, new revelation, and rebirth.

We know as Christians that spirit is indestructible. But if *I* don't know the power of the Holy Spirit first hand, if the spirit is not breathing within **me**, my identification will be with form. Reformers will come, prophets will come, artists will come, mystics will come, and they will continue to point out to people that the form, in and of itself, profits nothing. *It is the spirit that gives life.* The people who are encapsulated in form will kill the prophets because they don't know the spirit. Their identification is with the crystallization of the form. The form is for them an entity to be preserved, rather than the tomb it has become.

The fundamental task of change is to lead people back to a spiritual existence, to an existence that is alive with the fire of the spirit — to an existence in which the Spirit illumines all things. It's what Christ did with the religion of his time; it's what Luther did with the Catholicism of his time. The church had become lost in the relics, the indulgences, and other practices of the time. The church had lost its spirit. It had lost God. Luther challenged the church to rediscover its spirit. This is the heart of the reformation.

The heroic journey is the journey to the spirit.
It's a journey to the source of energy.

Chapter 4

Spirit In Form

The glory of the Incarnation is that God took form, the Word became flesh. The task of Christianity is to see through that form to the divine. Humanness, flesh and bones, gave Jesus visible, touchable form, but were that form not filled by the Spirit of God, it would count for nothing. The flesh profits nothing. Form that is permeated with Spirit is sacramental. Jesus Christ is the ultimate sacrament, the ultimate form, the prototypal form that reveals the spirit of the Creator.

Life is a constant interplay between spirit and form. I refer to this interplay as a dialectic. There is a constant dialectic between form or law or structure, and spirit. Our emotions are expressed through our bodies. When we feel things inside, we manifest them externally; we cry, we scream, we fight, we whisper. Our bodies are themselves the expression of an idea. The inner world always moves to the outer, and when the outer world replies, we take that reply deep inside ourselves where we formulate a response. Our own thoughts spring from an ineffable, invisible, inexhaustible source deep within us, a source that we can neither see nor touch. We know it only in its manifestations: our thoughts take flesh in our words, our songs, our dance, our culture. We are spirit in form.

This is the first principle. We simply cannot survive without form. The chaos brought on by change occurs when the form is disturbed, altered, or even removed. If we don't have sufficient strength of spirit, are not adequately grounded or centered in God, if we don't at least have access to the spirit when the form is being taken away, then we are bound to fear for the very future of ourselves.

Forms take on a life of their own. Consider the development of an embryo within the uterus of a woman. Imagine the fertilized egg being nurtured and nourished and protected by the womb. In response to that nourishment, the fertilized egg grows. As an embryo, then a fetus, it pushes that form out to its furthest limits, until finally, something decisive happens. The form that until now has been nourishing and life-giving, becomes life-threatening. *The womb has become a tomb.* At that point, change must occur.

That passage from womb to world is the initial heroic journey. A newborn infant must push its way through a life-threatening passage, in order to avoid death. There is the threat of death in the birthing process, but death is inevitable if the baby remains in the womb.

That process of a form supporting us, then imprisoning us, is the substance of life. It is "the curse" of life. We move into forms; we fill out that space and after a while, in one way or another, we've outgrown it. Not too long after the birth of a baby, that child is testing new limits. It breaks out of the womb in order to get into the home, but soon the home becomes too confining, and s/he must break out into school. Some years later, the school must be abandoned only to be replaced by other forms. This pattern continues throughout life. I have come to the realization in my own life that *the search for happiness is, in fact, a search for forms that work. Unhappiness comes because the forms in our lives are not working.*

It's possible, on the other hand, to have too much spirit and never to arrive at a workable form. One can perpetuate chaos for the sake of chaos, and I believe that to be as unhealthy as a too rigid attachment to form. There are times when the form should not be changed. There may be times when it should be renewed, rejuvenated, or re-affirmed. Lack of perseverance can be just as detrimental and dangerous as the refusal to hear new ideas.

Sometimes when we run into a conflict, instead of digging in and resolving it, we abandon the effort altogether. Statistics tell us that an extraordinarily high percentage of couples who lose a child to death end up in divorce. One reason for that frightening statistic might be they are not willing or spiritually equipped to stay with the struggle.

Every breakthrough
entails first of all a breakdown.

I will never forget the moment I understood the phenomenon of "Positive Disintegration." A lecturer at the Menninger Clinic in Topeka, Kansas, was describing independent findings by psychiatrists in both Poland and the United States. The observation was that when people go through major changes, they necessarily go through a period of disintegration. But if they stay with the process, if they go through it rather than around it, the disintegration turns out to be positive. The speaker went on to explain that every act of creativity is preceded by a breakdown of an earlier way of thinking. Every breakthrough, he said, entails first of all a breakdown.

I remember being thunderstruck! Despair, craziness, questions of faith are all part of the process! The pain of disintegration is necessary in order for reformation to occur, and it occurs to some extent every time a form is no longer workable. Human beings thrive in forms that work—family systems, work places, and churches that are working. When our operative forms are working well, life is usually calm and even joyful. When they aren't, we are in *dis-ease*. I used to believe that life was essentially a search for self, but no longer. I now think life's search is for forms that are working.

Let me share an example of what happened in my own life. Our third child, Bill, was four years younger than his brother and sister.When it came time for him to go to high school, he decided not to follow them into the parochial school, but chose instead to attend public school. Once there, however, he seemed to get lost in the larger school. He looked for smaller, more easily entered circles, but he discovered his peers had already formed themselves into cliques.

Bill found his form in a skateboard. Skateboarding for him became not just a pastime or "leisure activity;" it was a form for his life, an identity to which he could attach. He began skateboarding up and down the block, and soon he asked if he could put a quarter ramp in our driveway. Before we knew it, we had a bunch of other skateboarders in our driveway. Then he asked for a half ramp, and he built a half ramp. Before long we had young people from all over the city coming, and they were very different from the friends who had frequented our home before. They had green hair and orange hair and spiked hair and an odd assortment of clothing styles, and, in most cases, they were older. Yet they offered Bill acceptance and friendship, a place to belong.

For a time, Bill became part of that group, and because they were somewhat older, he began to live ahead of himself. We worried, and we monitored what pieces we could control, but all his mother and I could really do was to tell him, "Bill, we love you and someday you'll find your way."

His grades began a downward slide, which probably didn't make him any happier than we were. He was adrift in this lifestyle, searching for a more suitable form, but unable to find one that worked. We were doing our best to help, but all we could really do was to be there for him.

One day, as he and I were shooting hoops in our back yard, he said to me, "Dad, I just can't find my place."

We learned of a college in New York where a young person could bypass the junior and senior years of high school and move right into college, and Bill made application. But just at this time, one of his high school teachers asked him to join the academic decathlon team. For this he would have to meet with the team three hours every night, then go home and study ten different subjects on his own. He agreed to the challenge, and we began to see a different person. He began to talk about other students with whom he had previously felt nothing in common, as new friends. He talked over supper about economics and sociology. He was suddenly alive. He had found his place within the system, and he was ignited by its challenge. Needless to say, he withdrew his college application. He had found his form.

Once when I told the story of Bill in a presentation, a father spoke to me afterward relating that his son had lost a leg in an accident. With his new identity, he was forced to let go of all that had previously worked for him. In his desperation, he found he could ski with one leg, and he gave himself completely to the pursuit of this new identity. As he transcended his disability, he found a new confidence in himself and, with that, a whole new existence.

We are all at times in a search for form. The countries of the former Soviet Union are searching desperately for forms that work. South Africa is experimenting with forms in a search for one that works. Many women are demanding a form, a socio-economic order, that works for them. Minority groups are struggling to find a form for themselves.

So the church must be constantly searching for a relevant form. What our parishioners are looking for is a form that works *for each of them*, a form that allows them to express their spirits, and at the same time gives structure to their spirituality. They must feel in their own minds, hearts, spirits, and bones that worship (and the church as a whole) provides an end to the search. Form must nurture spirit. *Change is a restlessness around forms that fail to nurture the spirit.*

The Necessary Emptiness

What is it in nature that, having created the forms, always wants to then discard them? What are the roots of this "curse" we live under? We operate in an endless life-cycle, setting up systems only to have them lose their usefulness. Wombs become tombs, and we're called once more on the heroic journey, once more to the adventure of artistically and creatively reconstructing our lives.

I believe that if we trace this dynamic back far enough, we come face to face with the origins of evil. *The basic purpose of evil is to perpetuate forms that are self-serving rather than liberating.* Evil purpose insists, "I'm holding on to these destructive forms at all cost, regardless of how destructive they are." The opposite of this persistent, egocentric pattern is the humility or emptiness that accompanies an open, receptive stance, wherein we empty ourselves of form when it is time to do so.

In 1958 I found myself in Innsbruck, Austria, studying under a great Catholic theologian named Karl Rahner. This man shook the very pillars of my mind and reshaped my theology and my basic understanding of life. But before that could happen, I had to empty myself of all I had held as truth. Until then I had seen God as "out there," but I began to understand with brilliant clarity that God is also "in here," within the human heart. I saw that the Spirit of God moves from the inside out. I understood that the action of the Spirit is to move us from within, out to an encounter with reality. Life is a continuing interplay between spirit and reality, and it is meant to be lived from the inside out.

When emptiness occurs in the change process, we experience the discomfort of Holy Saturday or the fifty days of waiting in the Upper Room. We are forced into a period of advent in which the old has gone, but the new has not yet come. William Bridges in his book, *Transitions*, calls this stage "the neutral zone." (*Addison-Wesley, 1980*) It is an unavoidable period of gestation, a season of winter, which cannot be abandoned before the arrival of spring. We experience all the characteristics of Advent, the longing and yearning for the coming of the Messiah, a coming of illumination, direction, inspiration.

It is my experience that the inspiration will only emerge in an attitude of solitude and peace. Anne Morrow Lindbergh said "You lie open, choiceless, on the beach waiting for the gift from the sea." (*Vintage Books, 1959*) It is a characteristic of the spiritual life to be watching and waiting, expectant, but powerless, waiting, waiting. According to Karl Rahner, the best we can do as human beings is to become receptacles, listeners, harkeners for the word...waiting for grace.

Then, it happens. The inspiration comes, and the way becomes clear. We experience a Pentecost. As the followers of Christ, after fifty days of utter confusion, finally understood the suffering Messiah, so we are given a new understanding of God's will...and the courage to fulfill it.

Chapter 5

Transformation Of Consciousness

On the road to Damascus, Paul came truly to understand Jesus as the Christ, the fulfillment of Pentecost. With the outpouring of the Spirit came the promised, doubted, long-awaited understanding. An elation took place as the new finally came into consciousness. It was a new day, a new dawn, and the energy surrounding this event would become invincible. Paul knew what he was about to do, and it didn't matter if he might be killed doing it! He understood now what it was all about!

Now, the inspiration becomes what Campbell calls "the boon" of the journey. The boon is the new perspective, the new revelation. It is the transformation of *consciousness*. E.E. Cummings wrote, "I who have died am alive again today." He talks about how he saw the trees and the sky differently. "Now the eyes of my eyes see and the ears of my ears hear." *(Harcourt Brace, 1926)* It is the moment of revelation, of knowing.

With change comes the creative task of taking this inspiration and molding it, sculpting it in what I call *the organizing principle of the new form*. One now must go forth as the creator called to task. In change we experience a double progression, first letting go of old forms and moving out into the desert, and then, after receiving the new vision, returning to the charge of reformation.

This process of reforming has its own dynamics, and in the metaphor of the journey, it is what Campbell refers to as *the return*. Some people refuse to return. They elect instead to remain in the inspiration phase. Much more mystic than artist, I prefer the informational stage. When people asked, "Have you written your book yet?" I had to say, "No, I haven't written the book yet. It's too hard to put it together." While we may be more fulfilled in the state of receiving the inspiration, we are nevertheless called to embody it and go on. Tempting and gratifying as it may be, no one can stand empty, formless before God forever. Change is a process of creation.

Change is always a descent into death and those who are too afraid of death will not change. Unless a person first loses his or her life, that person cannot find it again. "Very truly, I tell you, unless a grain of wheat falls into the earth and dies, it remains just a single grain; but if it dies, it bears much fruit."*(John:12:24)* In Christ we have the physical manifestation of the mystery of birth, death, and rebirth.

The application for the church is at the same time simple and complex. Simply speaking, when a church is over-identified with form, it cannot remain that way and live. It *must* be renewed. When Jesus encountered the religious leaders of his time, he was battling an institution that had become over-identified with form. *The church must always be reformed,* and in order to do that, the church itself must continually follow the lead of its master into death. This is where it becomes complex. We must continue to give up forms that are stagnant and no longer challenge us, in order to touch and be touched by the Spirit.

A Safe Environment

The journey of change often leads us through despair. Human beings, with their utter passion for form, are nevertheless required by circumstances to regularly give up old forms. People are terrified of non-form, but they must go through the stage of chaos and emptiness, in order to come out the other side. For this journey we need a container to hold us together. We need a safe environment.

The container or vessel for this journey can be a pastor, a true friend, a therapist, or a support group, anyone who is known to be safe. "Safe" in this context means we will not be put down for any of the pain of the journey or hurried along in the process. It is imperative that we are with people who are not afraid of themselves. Ministers, ordained and lay alike, heal best out of their own despair. *They know despair and can therefore allow others to go through it.* In that process, we are not told what to do; we are not controlled or manipulated. Finally, in the security of a safe environment we will risk speaking our truth.

First, we risk *thinking* our truth; then we have the courage to share it. In my own experience, the truth proceeds in three levels. First, as we find ourselves safe, we begin to feel safe to tell another what we think. That means we can disagree. It means that I understand you don't think what I think. I am not you and you are not me. When we have safety in the head, I've found, the whole system begins to warm. The warmth creeps down into my chest and heart, and I begin to open up and feel safe to tell you not just what I think, but what I feel.

We can all be heroes as we adjust to the living and dying of life.

I dealt with a couple some years ago whose child was thought to have terminal cancer. The husband had grown silent and withdrawn and the wife said, "Talk to me, talk to me."

He said, "I won't!"

"Why won't you talk to me?" she asked.

He answered, "It goes too deep; don't do it, don't challenge me."

She grabbed his face with both hands and cried "Speak to me! We can lose our child, but I will not lose you!"

"I can't!"

"Talk to me!!"

"All right, I'll tell you. I want to get the hell out of here!"

And she said without hesitation, "Right! So do I, but you're not going, and I'm not going, and we're going to talk to each other."

"You mean you want to get out of this marriage, too?" he asked.

And she answered, "You're damn right!"

With that, it was out. They had shared their despair. Later they told how their marriage went through this metamorphosis. Having once begun to open up, they were not afraid of disclosing the rest to each other. Flowers when put in cold water will close, but if they are placed in warm water, they open. Place us in a safe environment and we open up as well. We will risk sharing and opening our hearts. That is the second level of safety. As the water gets warmer, the safety seeps down into our belly and into our bones and we begin speaking the truth from our bones. This is the third and deepest level of safety.

In my work as a therapist and "guide," I tried to create a safe environment for an orthodontist to work through abandonment by his wife. I was able to walk with a farmer through the very difficult process of closing out his farm. I consoled a woman in her forties who was diagnosed with a terminal illness and mourned with a couple who had lost their child. Over and over again, as I watched these heroes, I realized all they needed was a safe environment in which to open up. Always there was, "Oh, I thought you'd think this was foolish," or "Oh, I was determined not to cry." And I would tell them their tears were sacramental. "Allow the tears to heal you."

As I watched these people, they became heroes to me. We can all be heroes as we adjust to the living and dying of life. These heroes could take the tragedies of life and death, and could somehow go right through them, emerging on the other side in a rebirth, miraculously *transformed consciousness*. They actually saw life differently. While they would agree that they would not wish this agony on anyone else, they also acknowledged that it was simultaneously the worst and best of life's experience. Inevitably, they became aware of what was really important. In the future, *and in the here and now,* they would inevitably live differently. They would live more conscious lives.

Fiddler On The Roof

I know of no better portrayal of the passage from one form to another than the play and movie, *The Fiddler on the Roof*. Recall with me this classic presentation of change about Tevye, a dairy farmer in the small Russian town of Annitevka. As the play opens, Tevye spots a man fiddling on a roof top and comments, "Ah, the fiddler on the roof, that's what each one of us is, trying to scratch out a pleasant, simple tune without breaking our necks." Is there a better metaphor of our human predicament?

"And how do we maintain our balance?" Tevye asks. "Tradition! One word, tradition!" Traditional forms hold us together. They keep us safe. They create identity, and provide predictability and the assurance of expectation. They are the ground of trust and confidence.

One of the traditions in Annitevka is that of matchmaking. Tevye and Golda his wife have three marriageable daughters, and through them the conflict between that traditional form and the new paradigm of marriage for love is played out in increasingly painful ways.

Change always invokes conflict. The new invariably clashes with the old; the antithesis confronts the thesis. Change happens with the introduction of new information. New information is generally met with denial or disbelief. Simply because the new is new, it requires a period of adjustment before it can be interpreted, understood, and integrated into the old form. Tevye's response is typical, " Zittel has pledged her love to Mottel the tailor? Why that's absurd! It's impossible!"

In the case of his first two daughters, Tevye does an interesting thing. He finds a safe environment, and with God as a guide, he fiddles through his ambivalence; he reasons with his God, just as we all must do when the time of decision is at hand. "It is absurd. But, on the other hand, she loves him." In the end Tevye comes down on the side of the new idea. He too chooses love over tradition, spirit over form.

When finally his youngest daughter, Havela, pushes him beyond his limits by falling in love with an enemy Czarist, gentile soldier, Tevye fiddles again. This time he decides to come down on the side of tradition, saying, "I can bend, but I cannot break." He forbids her to marry and threatens to disown her if she does.

Havela now must do some fiddling of her own. She chooses love and accepts the inevitable death her decision entails, the death of her relationship with her parents and of her entire tradition.

This painful experience of death and grief is a turning point for Tevye. Through watching his daughters pursue love at the cost of riches, home, family, and tradition, a critical shift has taken place deep inside him. He turns his attention inward and begins his own heroic journey. Allowing the question to surface from deep within, he approaches Golda to ask, "Do you love me?"

The new idea has now arrived home with full force. The issue is no longer "out there" with his daughters; *it is now personal to Tevye himself. It is intimately and deeply his own.* When after much resistance Golda finally says, "Yes, I love you," Tevye responds, "And I love you!" In that moment their marriage is transformed from a marriage of tradition to a marriage of consciously expressed love. The center of their relationship has shifted. It will never again be the same.

The final victory of spirit over form occurs at the end of the play. Annitevka has been destroyed in a pogrom, and her citizens are dispersed abroad. As Tevye and Golda are preparing to leave, Tevye calls to his eldest daughter, "Tell Havela to call when she gets to the new country!" Now the transformation is complete. The old order has died, and the new form is born. Love will hold supremacy over form. Tradition will become a *living* tradition, always open to reformation.

Chapter 6

Consciousness Precedes Being

In my work as a consultant to organizations in change, I often find myself facing the same phenomenon: *a fixation on program, structure, and personalities, and a blindness to the power of the spirit of the people.* Chief executive officers, department heads, or deans decide to reorganize or restructure, and they, with a little help from some close associates, write a strategic plan. When the plan is finished, everybody nods, they put the plan on a shelf, and they return to the caldron of chaos and mistrust they had hoped to escape. Either they have never addressed the inherent resistance to change issue, or if they have, they expect it will take care of itself over time.

Vaclav Havel, the first president of Czechoslovakia after the overthrow of communism, is a hero of mine. He delivered an address to the United States Congress which was so powerful it brought hardened senators and congressmen and women to tears. Havel asserted that "*consciousness precedes being, and not the other way around.*" He went on to say, "For this reason, the salvation of this human world lies nowhere else than in the human heart, in the human power to reflect, in human meekness and in human responsibility." *(Time/March 5, 1990)*

As I read the speech in *Time* magazine, I was thrilled and overwhelmed. Someone had actually spoken the words in our halls of government. *Consciousness precedes being.*

Jesus said basically the same thing. "The Spirit gives life; the flesh counts for nothing." *(John 6:63NIV)* All evil and goodness, and even the salvation of the world, are hidden in the souls and hearts of people. Only there are answers revealed. Through prayer, through communion with God in the presence of the Spirit, life is given form.

I find in my work with organizations that this concept is not easily grasped. Most organizations function as though being precedes consciousness, that somehow we can successfully strategize before we understand and trust one another.

> The Spirit of the Living God is all about
> touching the human heart.
> Worship forms...and programs that work
> are the outer manifestations of inner grace.

Change is that call to consciousness, to the spirit. It's a constant call to relearn who we are because God doesn't ultimately care about our forms. God doesn't care about whether the Lutheran church, the Catholic church, or any particular denomination survives in its present form. That's not what the Creator of the universe is about. God is about holiness and wholeness. The universe is all about people seeking God, compassion, forgiveness, understanding, praise, adoration, and contrition. The Spirit of the Living God is all about touching the human heart. God, our Creator, cares about our consciousness, our spirit. It's not that forms are unimportant. "Do you think that I have come to abolish the Law or the Prophets; I have come not to abolish them but to fulfill them," (Matthew 5:17NIV) that is, to enliven them with spirit.

To the extent we give ourselves away to form, we are slaves. We may give our best to our families, but we may not give ourselves away to our families. We may give ourselves to our careers, but we may not give ourselves away to our careers. The first commandment is to love God with our whole heart, our whole soul, and our whole mind. And only then are we to love our neighbor as we love ourselves. "Martha, Martha, you are worried and upset about many things, but only one thing is needed... Mary has chosen what is better, and it will not be taken away from her."*(Luke 10:41-42NIV)*

In this age of "busyness" and running from solitude, we run after forms. We tell ourselves that if we cling to the form, we can take our rest. Or if we change the form, we can finally rest. If we restructure the church from this to that, it will grow or at least survive. But restructuring is not the only answer. Not until we first touch one another in the spirit, not until we first hear and respect each other, will we together create worship forms, liturgies, rituals and programs that work *because* they are sacramental. They are the outer manifestations of inner grace. It doesn't work the other way around. *Strategic plans do not necessarily lead to a sense of community, but if one creates community, strategies will unfold.* This has been my experience repeatedly.

And so continues the dialectical dance between form and spirit. We are happiest when the forms of our lives are outer expressions of our inner souls. If I take a walk with a friend among the trees and the beautiful birds, with the river flowing nearby, and I say to my friend, "How are you doing?" it's his invitation in a totally safe environment to talk about his work or his life, and I may just listen. I, in turn, can say the most embarrassing things in the world to him. The flow of energy protects. It's as if we're playing a duet on the piano. Time passes, and we don't feel fatigue on the walk. There is a perfectly safe flow of energy because love has cast out fear.

That same day I may meet another who I suspect is far more interested in my station or my credentials than what is on my heart, and I know instantly that I'd better be careful about what I say. It's all mask, persona, form. I know immediately when

I enter some environments that everyone is uptight. The rules of the organization are felt to be more important than the persons they were designed to guide.

Joseph Campbell used to say that the most important things he learned could be put in four words: "transparent to the transcendent." *(Doubleday Bell Publishing Group, 1988)* When things are transparent to the transcendent, we don't need to ask any more "why?" questions about life: *Why* suffering? *Why* did evil come into the world? *Why?* All those questions fall away because we have experienced an epiphany; we have seen the radiance of God's presence in a person or a sunset. We've known it in a moment in time. Those experiences are sacramental. They are penetrated with grace, with life, and with light. They are self-authenticating.

If we're not willing to descend to the spirit in the process of change, reform is no more than tinkering.

While my wife and I were vacationing recently in California, we went to King's Canyon. The road winds down and around for 30 miles, and at every bend the views change. At the bottom we found a magnificently beautiful brook with the clearest water rippling over the rocks. This experience was for me a metaphor of the heroic journey, as we travel down and down into our most beautiful place, the center of our souls. The arrival is such ecstasy, we want to remain there the rest of our lives. Surrounded by exquisite beauty, we dip into the rippling, singing water, which is the spirit. We descend all the way down to the center of our being in order to drink from the pure water. If we're not willing to descend to the spirit in the process of change, reform is no more than tinkering.

The question is, how do we make the forms transparent to the transcendent? How do we transform our churches, the liturgy, the preaching, the sacraments, into an epiphany? That transformation (or the hunger for it) is why people come. If they don't receive it, they will not stay. They will continue to search until they find it. I believe it's just that simple.

Those who do stay on are either being fed somehow or they are simply locked in form, and if it's the form that has their allegiance, they will feel very insecure when the winds of change begin to blow. We are called to freedom, but if we believe people really want freedom, we may have to re-examine that opinion. I am reminded of a line by Jack Nicholson from the movie, *Easy Rider,* that went something like this, "You think the people don't like you because of your long hair, but the real reason they don't like you is because you're free. "

> How tragic it would be if the church itself were to become the guardian of the forms rather than the guarantor of the spirit.

We will only allow others to be as free as we are. So, if pastors or parish leaders have not found within themselves the freedom to dance and sing, if the spiritual life is not being nourished, then change will most likely be a simple realignment of forms. It will not get to the heart. The great teachers and prophets of all denominations and all time have pleaded with us to live in form, to even dance in form, but to place our allegiance with the spirit. It is the spirit that abides through all change and if we place our allegiance with the spirit, then and only then will we reach the peace the world can't give.

I believe *the quintessential mission of the church is to be the safe place in society, where the primary allegiance is always to God, where there is no vested interest in anything but the love of God.* In the confines of the church, we are safe to hear where the Spirit leads without regard for form or for vested interests. *How tragic it would be if the church itself were to become the guardian of the forms rather than the guarantor of the Spirit.* At that time then, the prophets will reappear and call the church back to its original mission and purpose. The church started at Pentecost and is driven by the Spirit, and when it loses sight of that and becomes rigid, it needs to hear the call to adventure and to journey down through its own death and rebirth. The fundamental act of spiritual conversion is the shift of the mind and heart from allegiance-to-form to allegiance-to-spirit.

> The fundamental act of spiritual conversion is the shift of the mind and heart from allegiance-to-form to allegiance-to-spirit.

We are invited into conflict in order to become conscious, to take ownership of the subjective process. When we are fully conscious, no transformation is too difficult. It is our ethical responsibility to create for ourselves a desert, a mountain top, a rain forest, a place apart, an inner church in which to commune. For it is in communion that we gain the sense of safety, of peace, power and direction, and a joy that the world can't possibly understand.

The call to change in the church is first and foremost a call for the church to retouch its spirit, to renew its consciousness of itself. To be on the cutting edge as a church, I believe we must be holy.

Part II

Processing Change

Chapter 7

A Safe Place And Freedom To Risk

Change is both a noun, "a process or result", and also a verb, "to modify or substitute," which impacts our inner consciousness. No one is immune to change. In a discussion of change, we can't simply consider change as an external event or set of circumstances. In order to change successfully, we must also see change as an experience.

Each of us must process that interplay between the objective change out there in the world and the inner change implications as they affect us personally. How do we approach new paradigms? How long does it take to catch an idea? How do we protect ourselves? Everyone reacts according to whatever style has served in the past. What is your style when change hits you? Do you get sick? Do you move out too fast or become resistant? What is your own subjective experience of change?

In my early 30s I made a very difficult career move. In the process I got stuck in the murky waters of change. The first thing I learned about navigating those waters was the power of ambivalence. I wanted to "have my cake and eat it too." I wanted to give up my former life and to hold on to it at the same time. In that experience of ambivalence, I was trapped between the call to the new and the familiarity of the old. I was in a form that worked for me in the sense that I knew how to do it, but I was hearing a call to move on.

In my anguish I knew I needed help, so I sought guidance from a professional who provided what I later came to understand as a "safe environment." In the safety of his office two

71

hours each week, I realized over a period of time that he was relating to me in a way I had not experienced before. This man basically just sat there and listened empathetically. He didn't really seem to care what I might choose to do. He told me I had the answers inside myself, and that I would have to experience all the "stuff" locked within my head, heart, and bones. He told me that when I had finally released all that was knotted up in me, I would be clear about what I wanted to do and where I wanted to go. Out of my chaos would come clarity.

In the movie, *Ordinary People*, Connie began to see a therapist after the drowning death of his brother. It took many visits before the young man was finally able to name the fury he felt toward his brother for having drowned. With that anger came forgiveness, and with forgiveness, a new source of fresh energy. His life once again began to move forward.

Like Connie, I was not used to crying. I had learned early to control my tears, as "boys do." I had to re-learn to deal with the grief that was attached to my paralysis. I had also learned long before that men "aren't supposed" to be afraid. But in fact, I was terrified. I didn't know I *could* be angry. I had been taught that anger is "a mortal sin," but I soon understood that anger is often necessary before forgiveness can be felt.

I learned to trust myself more because I had come to trust my guide and because he trusted me. I became more real and increasingly more honest with him. Eventually I learned to be honest with myself. He encouraged me to show anger, to cry, to express fear. He held everything I said as sacred, and in the safety of his acceptance, I began to heal.

Then one day it happened. I found clarity. Previous sessions had ended promptly at the end of the hour. Sometimes I would be in the middle of a conversation when he'd say, "We'll have to continue this another time." On this particular day, twenty minutes remained on the clock. I had run out of things to say and was prepared to leave. He told me it wasn't yet time. Somewhat puzzled, I looked at him and asked, "What should we talk about now?" He looked back at me and said, "What do you *want* to talk about?" The question hit me like a wet dish rag.

I didn't know how to answer him, and it frightened me. I said, "I thought we were here to talk about what I *should* do, not what I *want* to do."

He answered, "Maybe that's the reason you're paralyzed. Maybe you're paralyzed because you're too tied up in 'shoulds,' the projections of your parents, family, and supervisors, and you've not yet gotten down deep enough inside yourself to know what you *want* to do."

I asked, "Are you giving me permission to do what I want to do?"

"No, no one can give that permission. *I can't give you freedom. The only thing I can ask you is why you don't take it?*"

I said, "If you're asking me what I want to do, there's no question about it. I *know* what I want to do."

"Why don't you do it?" He asked.

With that, all the barriers fell away. That night I dreamed of myself as a free man. From that day, I knew without question that a basic need in life is an environment in which we feel safe to be ourselves. We need to be able to process what is happening deep inside. The only way I know to process change effectively is to sit down with someone in a safe environment and to go through each phase, one step at a time.

When I did therapy with men and women who had lost their spouses, I would ask them to tell me about their spouses. They'd ask what I wanted to know, and I'd tell them anything at all. Inevitably, men and women who came in depressed began to open up and tell stories about their deceased wives and husbands. As they told their stories, they came alive. They began to cry and then to laugh as they recalled their times together.

They were able slowly to move ahead by reliving what those relationships had meant in their lives.

I worked with one woman whose husband died very suddenly in mid life. As a student of transition, she understood she had to go back before she could go forward. She decided to take her teenage children to her home state to show them where she and her husband were married, held their first jobs, and where the older child had been born.

While there, they became lost and ended up literally stuck in a cornfield. The boy in the back seat said, "Mom, this would not have happened if Dad were here, would it?" She recalled that at that moment, his death was upon them. She said the car turned cold and became like a tomb. The three of them sobbed, and she knew that was why they had come — to touch their pain and to release it.

They sat there washing away the pain in their tears. Finally the other child said, "Well, let's look at the good side. The one thing we know is we have to turn around." So they did.

She declared that night to be a party night, and told the children they could order pizza and stay up all night if they wished. She was going to get a bottle of wine, sit in the jacuzzi, and let go of this pain. From that time on, things went well. They saw everything they wanted and returned home renewed.

When she had finished the story, I asked, "Who was he to you? What did he mean to you?" She thought for a long time before she said, "Well, he was my lover, he was my husband, he was my business partner, and he was my best friend. He was everything to me."

I said, "So, what you have lost is *everything*." She nodded, "That's right." For her, *that relationship was everything* and with his death, *everything* was going to be different.

In the sadness that filled the room I said to her, "You know, I think you're still in love with him." She answered without hesitation, "I am." I told her not to give that up and she asked what I meant. I told her again not to give that up. "That's spirit, that's life, that's love. You don't give *that* up, you give up the form." That was a revelation for her.

A couple of weeks later she came back, and I noticed she wasn't wearing her wedding ring. She had always referred to it as "this damn wedding ring," and when I had asked her what she meant by that, she had said, "I can't take it off." I had told her the time would come when it would be okay.

In the course of the conversation that particular day, she held up her right hand to show me her remounted diamonds.

"Isn't it beautiful?"

"It's magnificent," I assured her. She held up both hands and said, "Chuck, I'm free."

About two years later she called and invited me to lunch. A wonderful man had come into her life, a gift. She told me she really felt free, and that the love for her first husband in no way interfered with this love. She had committed herself to releasing the pain and not allowing it to negatively affect her future. She did that by reliving her story. She understood how to process change.

One of the greatest joys I've ever experienced in my professional work was a series of workshops for pastors in southern Minnesota. The intent was to help them work with families during the rural crisis of the 1980s, which so greatly impacted every farming community. Nineteen priests and ministers were in attendance.

As we worked through the process, it became apparent something wasn't happening. We were bogged down, so eventually I stopped and asked, "What's going on?"

One of the pastors opened up and volunteered, "I can't continue talking about this because we are talking about the changes our parishioners are going through, and I'm feeling things welling up in me concerning my own changes." The others agreed to similar feelings, so we changed the focus of the workshop from helping *others* through change to processing change in *oneself*. These pastors shared with one another the pain and symptoms they were feeling. They were not trained to counsel people in such despair. They were feeling inadequate and burned out. Some were even thinking of leaving the ministry. The workshop became a textbook example of the heroic journey — *they stopped talking about others; instead they went inward. They began processing the changes going on within themselves.* They found in each other a support group that was sacred, and the time together proved to be transformative for many.

The church is to be a haven
where people can take off their masks...

The first necessary piece of the change process, then, is the establishment of a safe haven, a place in which any reactions we have are acceptable. In this safe environment, we have a chance to recapitulate the past...to recapitulate the meaning of the loss, the meaning of our resistance, our fear. We need an environment in which our spirits can be reborn.

In my estimation, this is what ministry is all about. The church is essentially a chrysalis, a safe, transitional object into which people can dare to come, to be who they are, express their feelings, and find acceptance. The church is to be a haven where people can take off their masks, find comfort in their pain, and then give birth to the spirit.

My business logo is my profession of faith. It shows a white dove flying out of a dark shadow into blue sky. That logo expresses for me my belief that it is only out of the darkness that we fly. It is only through the cross that we rise. The only way out is through. I believe that's the great teaching of Jesus. *But it requires tremendous maturity and courage on the part of the church to trust the human psyche, to trust that God is alive in the soul, and that our reactions to change are nothing more than a cry for freedom.* The gospel message is essentially that God is alive in each one of us. Salvation is in the spirit, not in the form.

Chapter 8

Regression
Recapitulation
Ritual

As I gained insight into the process of change through my own journey and those of others, it became increasingly clear that people will only be willing to go forward to the degree they are willing to go back. If one is not willing to go *all the way back to the beginning,* liberation will never be achieved.

The French have a saying for this situation, something to the effect that you have to draw back before you can go further. The idea is similar to leaping across a creek. More often than not, it can't be done from a standing jump, so, in order to make it across, one must backtrack a ways and take a running jump. The process I'm describing has three Rs to it: *regression, recapitulation, and ritual.*

Several years ago I was working with a corporate chief executive who had crossed the river of change long before but had left his troops stranded back on the other side. I related to him my theory that he would have to go back across the river, in order to gather his people, but he refused. He admitted he didn't have the patience or the time to go backwards. His words were something like, "We have to move to the future." He did, however, agree to send another person to bring the troops across. Six months later the executive was replaced by the person he had sent back to accompany the people.

William Bridges, in his wonderful book about transitions, *(Addison-Wesley, 1980)* talks about change being the external event and transition being the internal processing of the event.

We often bog down in the transition. I find many leaders are people with mighty vision who point across the river of great change and talk about wonderful possibilities, but they don't have strategies to help their people process the change. They don't prepare them for crossing the river.

I usually explain to them that if someone were to try to sell me a Porsche, that person could talk forever about how beautiful it is, but talk won't make me buy it. The more talk there is about its beauty, the more I'm turned off because I simply can't afford a Porsche. Until that person asks me where I am and what I'm interested in, *how much I can afford to pay*, I'm not going to come across the river to listen to talk about a new car.

So, as a leader, if you want to paint a vision across the river, don't begin talking about the vision. Instead, go back and listen to the people. Find out what they're willing to sacrifice and what they perceive the cost to be. It's a paradox you can't ignore.

When I work with organizations that are struggling with change, we first set the ground rules for discussion. We encourage the people to contract for safety, and in doing that, we identify whatever circumstances exist that militate against safety. It is critically important that everyone involved has an opportunity to fully express his/her reactions to what's happening without fear of reprisal or retaliation. They are far more likely to assent to change if and when they feel some ownership of the process.

Once the forum for safety has been established and people begin to talk about what's going on, at some point someone inevitably will say, "To understand what's going on now, we have to go back. You have to understand what happened here (say)three years ago." Another will add, "Well, this didn't begin three years ago, this began eight years ago." This *regression* seems to happen automatically. We always seem to want to go back before we can agree to move forward.

I believe we are called to live life three times: first, in anticipation; second, in actuality; and finally, in reflection.

The people instinctively begin to do a history of their relationship to the form. They're doing a *recapitulation* of their involvement with that form. Over and over again, in a variety of situations, the regression and recapitulation are necessary before a person is able to detach from the old form and move ahead.

I believe we are called to live life three times: first, in anticipation; second, in actuality; and, finally, in reflection. We look forward to an event in the planning stage; then we live it. Afterward we re-live it as we talk about the experience and come to some determination of what it meant to us and what memories we carry from it. It is in reflection that we become conscious. Then we can lay the past to rest. The failure to reflect can lead to the loss of soul. Interestingly, if one processes change well, reflection on the past precedes anticipation of the future.

Several years ago a new priest was assigned to a parish in a small midwestern town, where 100 years earlier German settlers had created a German parish. Six blocks away Irish settlers had created an Irish parish.

Over the years as the rural economy declined, the churches both began to suffer financially. They went to the Bishop and asked for money to keep their separate churches going, but were refused. Instead, the Bishop ordered them to merge and instructed the priest to begin the process.

Unfortunately, this task proved to be far more difficult than anyone had anticipated. The priest was repeatedly assaulted by hostile resisters. In fact, at one meeting they attacked him so mercilessly that he walked out of the meeting and out of the parish.

A new priest came in to the parish, and the resisters began attacking him in the same manner, but somehow he found strength to withstand. He dug down deep within himself, evoked the power of the Holy Spirit, and remained determined to introduce life-saving change.

Together with parishioners from each parish, he embarked on a four month period of recapitulation in each parish. With video cameras in hand, he and his lay leaders visited with the oldest people in the parishes and listened to their stories. When they finished that phase, they held a celebration in each church, recalling the glory and pain of their respective histories. When they had completed the celebrations in each parish, they closed one of the churches, and then, in a brilliant stroke, the pastor closed the other church as well. For six weeks they held mass in the school gymnasium, so that everyone could share in the loss.

Then it was time to reopen one of the churches. All of the parishioners from both of the previous parishes went out to the city park on a Sunday morning and had a picnic to celebrate their new community. After the Bishop blessed them, they marched in procession to the church, carrying certain altar pieces from the church that had closed. They ritualistically put the paraments into place in the "new" church. They were now a new community. That priest understood that in order to go forward, we need to go back. History must be validated before it can be released. If we don't complete the process of regression, recapitulation, and ritual, it will resurface as unfinished business.

Often the change agents of an organization are reluctant to reflect because they are action-oriented by nature. They think the recapitulation process might take too much time. I worked with a group of bankers who had merged seventeen banks, thinking the merger would be a great solution to the fiscal problems they faced. Their staffs, however, were enraged and confused because they didn't know what the new rules were. The presidents had the wisdom to sit down and talk about it.

One of them said, "Ah, Chuck, I don't believe in this recapitulation stuff. I think all you have to do is make up your mind to get on with your life. I know that because when my brother died, that's what I did."

I was pretty sure he would be rethinking that issue because my experience is that when you bury your reactions to change, they don't go away. In fact, they show up in symptoms like ill health, depression, addictions, interpersonal conflict. In our third seminar, this same executive came to me and said he had a story to tell me.

"I was out with my dog," he said, "and as I was throwing him sticks, the dog would go out and come back. I had just gotten into a rhythm, when suddenly the image of my brother came crashing into my consciousness. I broke down and sobbed. All the memories of my brother just flooded into my mind. I couldn't stop them.

"I feel cleansed now. If you had told me that I had all that inside of me, I would have bet you a thousand dollars I didn't. I had no idea I was carrying that unfinished business."

We live life in reflection. When we tell the story, we finally get to distill its meaning. Think about your experience listening to elderly people. They love telling their stories. My own sense is that often we do not encourage them far enough. "So, what did your life *mean* to you? What did you love the most? How do you wish to be remembered?"

They have more often than not been denied the opportunity to process their memories, to recapitulate and ritualize the joys and sufferings of their lives. We complete life in reflection.

When we tell our stories, we finally come to distill the meaning of our experience. We are then more open to change.

The Sacraments as Rites of Passage

Lately, I have become increasingly aware of the vital need for such rituals as a way of guiding people through the loss of old form. An *effective* ritual closes the lid, so to speak, on the old and opens the way for new life. After regression and recapitulation, we have a ritual, a rite of passage: a coming together of the community to celebrate the past, to tell its story and to lift it up into the present, say yes to it, and then let it go.

One goes back to tell the story, to discern the themes, and get down to the essence or the core. Only then is the ritual effective. A ritual without recapitulation is merely ritualistic. A ritual that does not take us in hand and lead us down through the change process is not yet a rite of passage.

Historically, the rites of passage provide a container for the transformation of consciousness. It is incumbent upon society to provide people with an ever-increasing number of those experiences. It is critical, for example, that children be welcomed in baptism into the family of Christ. It is critical for society that adolescents become adults, and to do that, they are led through the vision quests, which allow adult consciousness to emerge. It is critical that we have rituals around forgiveness, marriage, and mortality. When those sacraments are effective, that is, when they "work," they bring about a transformation of consciousness, walking us through death into higher forms of life.

The movie *Emerald Forest* describes a ritual of a native Brazilian tribe. When the boy, Tommy, reaches puberty, the elders of the tribe prepare him "to die." They anchor him in the water with only his head exposed, allowing insects to crawl over his unprotected face. Finally slipping into unconsciousness, he goes under as in baptism, submerged in the water of death. Then, as they rescue him from the water, they pronounce for all to hear, "Tommy, the boy, is dead! Tommy, the man, lives!" Such is the transformation of consciousness — too socially and personally important to be left to chance.

In our society, many rituals have become merely ritualistic. Have you ever been to a wedding that didn't work? In rituals that are effective rites of passage, one can immediately sense something special is about to happen. It might be the flutist, the candles, the flowers...it's hard to pinpoint exactly what it is, but one can immediately sense the spirit is present. People are individuated and cared for. You know at the time that the sacrament has become an effective sign of grace. It has achieved what it symbolizes, and you became part of the ritual. Rituals are celebrations of life which guide our spirits into community. The whole community experiences a lifting into a sacred level of consciousness. Every effective rite of passage is a Eucharist.

But what happens in a church or society where the rituals are no longer working? When baptism means little? Where confirmation doesn't signify transformation in any sense?

If we are looking for renewal in the church, I suggest we begin with our rituals. Are they truly transformative or are they merely ritualistic? If a pastor is too afraid of death, s/he is not ready to be a pastor because her purpose in that role is to guide people through death into new life. It is in the rituals that consciousness can be transformed, and the function of the church is to lead people through the various stages of that transformation into Christ consciousness...into adulthood, old age, into death.

Consciousness precedes being. Spirit precedes form. In our churches the music and the liturgies are symbols for the presence of the Holy Spirit. If we have music and liturgy, but not spirit, or no connection to the divine, the liturgy will be empty and devoid of life. People often go to therapists or to concerts rather than to church, in order to have a spiritual experience. When the church is no longer spiritual, when it's no longer transparent to the transcendent, all that links us together is form. Often we have forms that seem to be working on the surface, so our role becomes the mere perpetuation of those forms.

At one point in my teaching career, I taught a course dealing with loss and change. Thirty-eight people attended the first evening. As a way of introduction, I asked how many of the participants were going through a major change. Seven people raised their hands. As the quarter progressed and we identified the phenomenon of unfinished business, as we articulated the possibility of going through the change objectively but never really processing it subjectively, thirty-seven of the thirty-eight students eventually identified a major change they needed to complete. For example, one person had never let go of a past love relationship. Another had been laid off from his job, but had not let go of his bitterness. For many, it had to do with carrying around unfinished business from childhood.

One woman came to realize during our discussions that she had never buried her father. She now knew she needed to go through a regression, recapitulation, and ritual before she could be free. She told the class, "My father was a patient in a mental hospital when he died. I never knew why he was there or how he died. It was always kept secret by my mother. I went back to the hospital and asked if I could read my father's file, but was told I couldn't because my mother was still living. I then went to my mother and asked for her permission to read Dad's file, to which she replied, 'No, that's finished. I don't want to bring up those old ghosts again.'

"I feel I can't totally finish this business yet, but let me tell you what I intend to do. Someday, after my mother dies, I'm going back to that hospital to get my dad's folder and read it in detail. I'm going to try to figure out what kind of a person he was, what led him to be institutionalized, and how he died. When I have understood all that I can about him, I'm going to sit down and write him a letter. I'm going to take that letter to the grave and read him that letter. Then, I'm going to burn that letter, come back down that hill, and I'll be free."

Chapter 9

Three Basic Principles

Over the years I've identified three principles that continue to reappear in the sequence of change events. The first
principle is this:

**Change is never a neutral experence.
It always evokes strong reactions.**

*The biggest single mistake we make is to ignore the
experience of change by treating it exclusively as an event.*
What is decisive about change is not so much the event, but the
experience of it, how we respond to it. Mission, vision, plan of
action are all communicated as objective happenings in an
unattached world. Seldom does anyone bother to ask the
changees where they are with those changes or how they feel
about the fact they are in a form that is no longer working. "What
is your experience?" If no reaction is *felt,* nothing significant is
about to happen.

Where can we who are affected by change share our
reactions, our confusion, disorientation, our feelings of inad-
equacy? If someone has been serving the church for over forty
years, and then is told her way of doing ministry is no longer
relevant, what does that say about her as a person? What does
that say about the church? What does one say to a mother who
is told, in effect, that her advice is no longer helpful. In the call to
change self-esteem can be shaken.

I have personally found it hard to stay focused on the
experience of change. Instead I have habitually left my own
centering to follow the events. I have blamed others for my
inadequate responses to change. I have worried too much

about how others would perceive my reactions. I frequently edited my authentic experience to make it more acceptable, hid my anger or my grief. The challenge, I thought, was to adjust instantly to change, almost without reaction, rather than to recognize, much less reveal, what was going on in me.

It's time we get in touch with something besides our theology and our job descriptions. It is time to become conscious of something other than our heads.

When someone's heart is breaking, we need to be interested in that person's spirit, soul, not just in his or her ideas. The kingdom within is where the spirit lives, down deep inside. Carl Jung recalls a poignant conversation with an African chieftain, "You white men have such frowns on your faces. You think with your heads."

Jung looked at the man and asked, "Where else would you think?"

"You think in your heart. That's where you think." Every great artist and musician knows that. When the heart opens, the head will follow. Change affects us there in that open heart, and the experience is never without feelings attached. The reaction may well be positive, and it may be unexpected. It may be slight or overwhelming, disabling or empowering, temporary or permanent. Wherever change is happening, reactions are felt. Change is never a neutral experience.

The second principle is this:

If the reactions to change are not processed, they go underground and remain as unfinished business.

If the reactions are processed and interpreted into new consciousness, there is a flow of energy, a sense of well-being. But what happens when the flow is blocked? Unprocessed reactions to change pile up in the form of unfinished business. They gather shadow energy and finally reappear in the form of symptoms. Unfinished business may manifest itself in ulcers or headaches or a rash. It may come up in relationship conflicts, or bring on depression or even suicide.

Within an organization, a common set of symptomatology appears. It's the chronic, unending "whining, bitching, moaning, syndrome" in the coffee room. It's like a dark energy in the system, and the moaning and complaining takes on a life of its own. I'm not talking about the normal complaining. I'm referring to something immediately felt when someone walks in the door. It simply is a chronic negative energy that can't be ignored, like an elephant in the room. Everyone knows it's there, but no one feels free to talk about it. It's a terrible thing to have to face day after day.

Other operative symptoms might be absenteeism, turnover, or the loss of energy and creativity. The light goes out in people's eyes. Those who still come most likely do so out of obligation, but they're not on fire. Routine sets in. Ritualism replaces rituals. Dogmatism replaces doctrine. Pretty soon the load is too heavy to carry, "no one really cares; a few do all the work."

It takes discernment to see these as symptoms. What organizations, couples, families often try to do is to deal with the symptoms rather than uncovering their underlying cause. The journey from the symptom to the source of the unfinished business is part of the heroic journey. This heroic journey begins with the acknowledgment that we are stagnant, that we are polarized. It is the admission that some of us are still on the other side of the river, way back there, holding on to the past. Some of us are stuck, and in that stuckness, the gap is being filled by complaining or by name-calling or absenteeism, by the loss of spirit. The spirit has been lost and what is left is the form. What is left is the wasteland, the rock without water.

The reactions must be processed in a safe place, a place where people feel they can safely talk to one another, or they will inevitably continue to surface as symptoms.

The third principle is this:

There is no change that cannot be processed by the human spirit.

Regardless of how devastating the change may be, I believe the human spirit always has the capacity to heal. It is true that in some instances, changes can create a shock which is actually terminal, but if a person can get through the shock phase alive, any change can be processed with time.

The necessary process of doing that work is demanding, frightening, and heroic in nature. The heroic journey is, in my view, being willing to process what is happening to me, my subjective response to the objective conditions of reality. American psychologist William James believed this fact to be the greatest discovery of our generation: *by processing our own subjective reactions to reality, we can, in fact, change those realities.*

Ask yourself, then, how are you processing change? What mechanisms have you put in place to help those around you process what is taking place in their lives? If we as leaders are not willing to invest ourselves in that process, we are condemned to be trapped by form and symptoms. Change is inherent in growth. Renewal means death and new life.

Kirkegaard said, "We are condemned to freedom." *(Princeton, 1946)*We are condemned to claim that freedom or to deal with the symptoms that result from denying it. It just is that simple. *Consciousness precedes being, not the other way around.* This is nothing more than a variation of faith preceding good works. First, we become conscious, and then we build our world around that inner reality. First, we consciously become a community and then we develop strategy for that community.

In our organizations, parishes, families, if we develop programs or strategies without first building trust and mutual respect among ourselves, we will remain caught in programs. In scriptural terms, we are trapped in law. It's as if the program or the reorganization or restructuring is going to preserve us or save us. We think it's safer. It's not. My suggestion is rather to take the time to listen to the people now, to become conscious first, or we will take time later on to deal with symptoms.

Is the church taking a leadership role in helping people become conscious? Do we know who we are in a changing world?

Do we know who we are in a changing world?

Recently I dealt with a large corporation which had invested thirty million dollars in a manufacturing plant for the production of a particular aircraft engine part. Months after construction of the plant was completed, before any product had been manufactured, it closed due to the economic recession. During that time, the company had hired and relocated ninety-one people from all over the country, and now they were giving them seven additional months but with little or nothing to do. The employees had spent over a year developing a master plan which would never be implemented. I was called in to give a workshop intended to help them cope with these changes.

We decided I would guide all ninety-one people on a three-day journey through the death of their division. They agreed to work through the process of recapitulation.

We spent several hours in a large group, each person sharing his or her history with the company. After a long struggle, we reached the point where they were ready to express feelings, resentments, vanquished hopes and dreams, and to move ahead. We chose a ritual which called for each person to write down specific things that had to be discarded in order for them to move into the future. Once written, the papers and their contents were tossed into a huge trash barrel.

When that symbolic action was finished, we realized the ritual didn't go deep enough. After further discussion, it was apparent we were still not really treating it as a death, so the plant manager suggested holding a funeral and burying the master business plan. A cardboard box served as a coffin, and we walked in procession through the vast plant. Some people were talking but most were somber and reverent.

When the burial step was reached, they decided to burn their only copy of the master plan. They watched it go up in smoke, page by page. People were standing arm in arm, some crying, some joking, but everyone was engaged. And everyone agreed it was finally over.

The next day we returned to discuss what they might become as a temporary organization? What would be the new form? The consensus was to create a career development and placement center, each person committed to supporting each other in the job search. They would arrange for seminars, computer training, and brain-storming about job and career possibilities. The next day a sign was erected that read *Career Transition Center*. Aware they had created what amounted to a new master plan, they wrote a mission statement, rules and policies, and decided how they would celebrate when people began to leave. They had created a new community of profound impact to sustain them in transition.

Not What, But How

In the early seventies, I was in administration at a Minnesota state university. I had come in 1968 at a time when the university was on the rise. We were admitting students so rapidly we couldn't hire faculty fast enough to teach them. Our president predicted we would become a major university. We were on the rise.

Then the bombings in Cambodia began. With the escalation of the war in Vietnam, many faculty members, students and administrative staff began to hold "teach-ins" on campus, and before long, were marching downtown. On a fateful day for the university, the entire anti-Vietnam war group blocked the main downtown streets for four hours. The townspeople were outraged, and overnight we became known as the bastion of liberalism on the hill. Parents began withdrawing the students and transferring them anywhere "conservative patriotism prevailed." We fell into an immediate enrollment decline.

It's not so much what happens to us that is decisive.
Rather it's how we react to what happens.

That following year we began to eliminate positions, a few at first, but an increasing number each of the next two years. Cutting thirty positions by attrition was met with censure by the faculty, and on the heels of that move, I, as interim academic vice president, was responsible for reducing the staff by an additional twenty-five percent. I had no idea where or how to begin.

In that environment I made the most important administrative decision of my life. I refused to accept the problem as mine alone. I called the university community together and told them, "*We* have a problem; how are *we* going to solve it?" We invited faculty, townspeople, students, custodial staff, and alumni to join us in the process. "Circling the wagons" as a community, we decided together upon criteria for laying off people. We identified exceptions for those departments that might fit the criteria, but shouldn't be affected, such as minority and womens' studies. In the end the faculty senate passed unanimously a resolution praising the administration for "the thorough, humane and participatory manner in which the reductions were made."

That process was a profound experience for me, having seen the unpopular events of the previous year, and it taught me an important lesson: *It is not so much what happens to us that is decisive. Rather it is how we react to what happens. It's not the what; it's the how* .

If we approach change through the metaphor of a journey, change takes us away from the old and familiar, the part of us that has become old or stagnant, out into a desert, a void, a chaos, in which we are troubled. We go through travail until we reconnect with a vision. That vision is often a restoring or re-design of an old vision. The return portion of the journey is the artistic work of putting that vision into reality.

It is never really the change itself, but *our attitude toward change* that is crucial. The same change hitting two different people causes in one person an opportunity for growth, and another person a collapse into depression, possibly psychological death, and maybe even suicide. If we can't seem to get at the crux of the change by examining the action itself, then the real issue is the personal reaction to the change — our own heroic journey. We need a place to process what is happening deep inside.

How are we talking together? Who owns the change? Is it our peers, our constituents, society at large? Who owns the church or the organization involved? Who's driving the change?

It is possible to go through change *without really going*

through it. A study in California of people who were divorced showed that of the people surveyed, forty percent of the women and twenty-eight percent of the men were still angry at their ex-spouses five to ten years after the divorce was finalized. They went through the divorce without really *going through* it. They went through the external event of change, but they did not go through the internal processing of becoming a divorced person. I once counseled a woman who had been abandoned by her husband and left with three children. Sixteen years later that woman still did not see herself as "single." She considered herself "abandoned." She had never done the subjective work of change. The task of changing is inside.

The point then is that leaders in many organizations will come in and impose a change as an objective thing, not realizing the importance of helping people adjust to that change. It's called putting people in a double bind, like spanking a child, then telling the child not to cry.

Given a safe haven, people open to speaking the truth will automatically go back and begin telling their stories. As they go through the process, they will begin to understand what their experiences have meant and will come to this: "Look in your heart when you grieve, and you will find that what you grieve is what was beautiful." Rollo May says that without death there would be no beauty. We grieve what was beautiful. When we can touch that beauty, own it and name it, celebrate it, then we can let it go. What we take with us is the spirit.

Facilitating change in others means that we have to be willing to change ourselves. Only in our own state of transparency are we able to guide others into transparency. We will not lead people into greater freedom than we know ourselves. We cannot lead them into greater joy than we have felt.

No one can spare us the inner challenge of processing

change, for, "condemned to freedom," each of us is called to choose a false sense of security or freedom. Do you remember the Garfield cartoon about his experience in the pet store? Seeing all the pets in their cages, and feeling sorry for them, he opened the cages and cried, "Freedom, freedom, freedom!"

None of the pets moved an inch, so Garfield retraced his freedom walk, closing all the cages, saying, "Security, Security, Security!"

When the call sounds, we are all tempted to keep within the safety of fences. We are condemned to hear the call, or pretend we didn't hear it. Not to respond is to stay locked in form. We are condemned to freedom.

Chapter 10

Self-Care For Caregivers

Caregivers, professional or otherwise, are especially subject to front line isolation. Too many don't feel supported and have no place to go with the inevitable baggage. In my own ministry experience, my role was what Jung would call "a persona." It took me a long time to understand the wisdom of what he meant when he said we heal people out of our own wounds.

For example, alcoholism proved to be impervious to treatment by medical doctors or mental health professionals. It was only when a group of alcoholics came together to share with one another out of their own brokenness that healing began. I think that's the essence of Christianity: sinners sharing God's healing with one another. There is really no place in the church, much less in the ministry, for people who have not been wounded. Jesus didn't come for the well, but rather for the wounded. It's a strange but blessed paradox.

Conscious of our weakness, we reach out and heal, sharing our vulnerability in appropriate ways. We aren't asked to become inappropriately personal, but we must come down out of the role, into our own personhood in order to heal.

A strange phenomenon occurs when we share our wounds; others are invited to do the same. That's the secret behind all of the twelve step groups meeting today. Part of the heroic journey is to travel down inside and to touch one's vulnerability—that I don't have my own act together—that I am confused— that maybe I'm in despair. I am the same whether a superstar or a homeless drunk. Any assumed role or persona is shed, and my humanity is laid bare.

My wife taught me about the value of simple compassion some years ago. When she let me know, for example, that she had had a rough day, I invariably responded with a remedy I hoped would be helpful to her. But that wasn't what she needed or wanted. I continued for some time to assume the role of problem solver in an effort to take away her pain, while actually attempting to relieve my own discomfort in the situation. I asked myself, "What does this woman want?" Then one night I got it! Finding her a little down, I got up, walked around the table, and simply gave her a hug. You see, people don't need us to rescue them. Often they just need to be heard and consoled.

In our woundedness, we don't need someone to tell us what to do...
What we *do* need is tenderness...

In our woundedness, we don't need someone to tell us what to do, to intellectualize the situation, to rationalize it. What we do need is tenderness and compassion in that sacred setting of unconditional regard, and the only way that happens is by providing forums in which we can be vulnerable with each other.

If we don't have that safe place, where we can talk about our heads, our hearts, and our bones in a totally safe way, without being instructed or judged, there is no way we can heal others or be helped ourselves. That safe place can be with a friend or a spouse, or it may need to begin with a journal. Frequently, we find we are not safe with ourselves—that we edit our own "stuff." I'm not angry because I'm not supposed to be, etc. In fact, what we bring into consciousness is only what we think should be there, not always the full extent of what is really there. The safe place should be a safety bucket, in which we simply dump. The message of redemption purely stated tells us that problems can be worked through, and that God is ultimately alive in us. We can trust God.

Because the ultimate safe environment is created between two confidants, I have become a strong advocate of deep, one-to-one relationships. I believe that having one, two, or three totally real friends is a "sine qua non" of spiritual growth. If I am not transparent to one person who sees me as I am and loves me nonetheless, then in my view, my redemption is not finished. Being open and transparent before God is a necessary stage, but I must also be open and transparent before one other person, in order for my redemption to be incarnate. At least, so it seems to me.

> The call to the spiritual life is a call to empowerment—to effect changes in the world—but first a mandate for personal consciousness.
> *It is a call to know who we are...*

My sense of safety is that we read people intuitively; we automatically check each other out for safety. Is it safe for me to be real with you? We very quickly give and get signals from each other about how safe we are. When we're ready for that high level of transparency, the person will appear. If you want a transparent relationship with one other person, that person is available because this is in the order of redemption. You may first of all have to bring to consciousness your need for such a relationship. Then you'll be given the grace to ask for it, and then you will receive or achieve it.

If this safety can develop in a group, so much the better. My wife happens to be blessed with a group of four women friends who have a miraculous level of intimacy. It is not only therapeutic, but it has also created a level of wellness and emotional health that amazes me. At the same time, I've been blessed with three very close male friends with whom I share this transparency. It involves risk of self-revelation, but only that risk gives me the experience of mercy. This covenantal relationship is the only way I know to combat front-line isolation.

The call of the spiritual life is a call to empowerment—to effect changes in the world—but it is foremost a mandate for personal consciousness. It is a call to know who we are, to learn more and more, in an enlarged sense of consciousness, where we fit in the world, and who God is. There is a process of purification, so that the end result of tne heroic journey is a purity of heart, wherein God is present. God is both in the new and the old, in the dreams and the reality, in budgets as well as in the pulpit. "Blessed are the pure in heart, for they shall see God." (Matthew 5:8)

In the past, ministry training often failed to prepare a person adequately for the front lines. It consisted exclusively of theological content and homiletics. Even today one may not be trained in the process skills, in conflict resolution, or group facilitation. One of my best friends is a medical doctor. He told me that even in his training he never learned interpersonal care with patients or how to run a business, but only the content of medicine. There is little doubt that some day we may all need some professional leadership skills, negotiating skills, conflict resolution skills, group facilitation skills. It would be wise to prepare a personal development plan for two or three years in this area, embark on workshops, or to secure a mentor.

Finally, we have a responsibility to God and to those we serve to be renewed in our spirituality. Whether it's permission to escape periodically into music, to do a retreat off at the edge of the earth on a regular basis, or the discipline of regular meditation, we are called to spiritual growth and renewal. Music often does it for me. If I allow myself to tune into Mozart or Brahms, by the end of the first movement I'm generally into the music, and when I come back, my perspective has been restored. For other people, it may be a hobby— knitting, wood carving, nature, or the like.

I worked recently with a school district that was experiencing difficulties. In my set of recommendations, the word *forum* kept appearing. They hadn't provided forums in which they could work through their differences. They didn't have a mechanism to deal with their reactions to change. The Sabbath is such a forum. The rationale is that if we create the forum (keep the Sabbath), there is some hope we will develop the relationship (love God with our whole heart and soul). If we don't honor the forum, the agenda will devour us. If we don't create forums in which to renew ourselves with prayer, worship, song, nature, friendship, or with whatever it is that renews us, the soul withers and dies. It is unable to love.

To summarize, the first thing we need as individuals is transparency with at least one other person, a safe place into which we can escape for healing.

The second component has to do with the development of leadership, process, management skills in which we may never have been previously trained.

Thirdly, we must accept the ethical responsibility to honor our own Sabbaths, to create our own forums where we can renew ourselves on a regular basis. We are responsible for our own emotional, physical, and spiritual renewal.

Chapter 11

Community and The Holy Spirit

The final fruit of the spiritual journey is to be able to say with Paul, "it is no longer I who live, but it is Christ who lives in me." *(Galatians 2:20)* At Pentecost the disciples of Jesus were filled with the Holy Spirit, still today the supreme gift of the spiritual life. As I have studied and tried to understand the activity of the Holy Spirit in my own life and in the lives of the people I've been privileged to walk beside, I've noted four functions or purposes of the Holy Spirit in the human soul.

The first is to provide illumination, to point the way. The Holy Spirit clarifies what is going on, allowing us, in many cases, to see ahead and to understand. Secondly, the Spirit warms us with its presence. Jesus promised that the Spirit would comfort and console. The Spirit heals our wounds and prays within us when we don't know what to pray.

The third role of the Holy Spirit is to purify, to burn away the dross: our lies, fears, and egotism. The fire of the Spirit cleanses us. In the language of Jesus, the Spirit "prunes us," so that we can bring forth more fruit. Finally, the Holy Spirit unites us with God. We become channels, epiphanies of the spirit, through which the light shines and men honor not us, but the Creator who is at work in us.

The spiritual life has to do, then, with *illumination, consolation, purification and unification.* When we stay on our path, this is where the path will lead. This is true not only of individuals, but of entire congregations. The Spirit is what binds us all together.

We are becoming increasingly aware of the importance of creating communities in which differences are not pushed under the table, but are used rather to enrich the life of the congregation. Scott Peck describes a group that is conflict avoidant as pseudo-community. *(Simon and Schuster 1987)* True community honestly and openly faces and resolves conflict. It is inclusive of differences. It is rich in diversity.

I was brought up with the attitude that conflict was bad, and one needed to go to confession if one became angry or even entertained angry thoughts. The whole attitude toward anger or the expression thereof was negative. I now think we were missing the point. Jesus had no problem with anger or with conflict. He told us, in fact, that he came not to bring peace, but to cause conflict among families and communities *for the right reasons.* (Matthew 10:34,5)

The point is really about the fundamental attitudes surrounding conflict. Why is this painful to me? What is at risk? What do I lose by bringing conflict into the open? If I am willing to get involved in mediation, what must I be prepared to give up? How vulnerable am I willing to become for the sake of peace? These are the questions we have to consider if we are serious about an effort to bring reconciliation and create a sense of true community.

Conflict is painful to us for different reasons. Sometimes it requires the admission that the community in which we place our trust is cracked or crumbling. If we are to receive the gifts of a spiritual life unfolding in a safe and sacred space, we can't escape the reality of conflict resolution. A pseudo-community is only a shadow of the real thing. It is not worth protecting.

Conflicts are opportunities for creating community at deeper levels. For instance, if a family is suddenly faced with the experience of a disabled child, that child may become an occasion for the family to become closer than it ever was. If we consider a staff or parish problem to be a symptom of an underlying condition, we can be thankful for the opportunity to come together in a forum and talk about the underlying issues. What has gone unsaid? Discussion about an incident or a condition becomes a symbolic act around which we can unite to become more real, more honest, more open. All this is the work of the Spirit.

Chapter 12

The Three Phases

The Heroic Journey is a return to the spirit. It is living the spiritual life with an awareness that we are in charge of our agenda, the conflict, the forms that threaten to control our God-given freedom to commune. As the journey is archetypal, so the components of the journey are consistent. Let's examine these three phases: separation, initiation, and return.

Separation

The first is the separation from the old, which begins with "a call to adventure," as Joseph Campbell pointed out in his classic work, *The Hero with the Thousand Faces. (Princeton University Press, 1968)* The call to adventure is heard when life becomes too predictable or stagnant. It may come through sickness or a heart attack. It may come in the way of a threat to a marriage or as a job change. Something happens in life and is echoed in the soul, which clearly says that life in its present form isn't working.

Life wasn't working for a woman who came to my office for therapy. After we talked a while, I asked her, "Why did you come?" She said, "Because I woke up one morning and I realized my husband had not told me or shown me in four years that he loved me. When I came to that realization, I said to myself, 'I'm better than this. I'm made for more than this. I don't have to keep living like this." It was a call out of slavery to form.

The call can come in the form of a hunch, and it may come on quickly, without any preparation. Jesus described it as a wind that "blows where it chooses, and you hear the sound of it, but you do not know where it comes from or where it goes. So it is with everyone who is born of the Spirit." *(John 3:8)* If we are sensitive to a stirring in our bones and the depths of our souls, we begin to experience a whisper of something better, something more authentic, more fulfilling, more on fire.

We realize that somewhere along the way we lost the spark. We lost the glint in our eyes; we lost the dance in our feet; we lost the color, and, like Dorothy, we're living in a gray Kansas. If we choose to heed the call, it will bring pain to be sure, but if we ignore it, the dull ache of gray existence will eventually extinguish our spirit.

Robert Frost's wonderful poem "Mending Wall" summons one of the clearest pictures of a person refusing to hear the call to adventure. Frost lived on an estate in New England where he shared a stone wall with his neighbor. Every winter the wall would become packed with snow and ice, and in the spring, when the ice melted, the stones would tumble. Each year, Frost recalled, he would call his neighbor saying, "It's time to mend the wall again."

As they went out to the wall on one occasion, Frost heard something stirring within him. The thought occurred to him that they had gone through this ritual year after year, and maybe they were fighting against something that simply shouldn't be.

Something there is that doesn't love a wall,
That sends the frozen-ground-swell under it,
And spills the upper boulders in the sun;
He asked his neighbor, "Why are we building this wall back up again?"
There where it is we do not need a wall:
He is all pine and I am apple orchard.
My apple trees will never get across

> And eat the cones under his pines, I tell him.
> He only says, "Good fences make good neighbours."

At this point Robert Frost wrote my favorite line in all of poetry:

> Spring is the mischief in me, and I wonder
> If I could put a notion in his head:
> Why do they make good neighbours? Isn't it
> Where there are cows? But here there are no cows.
> Before I built a wall I'd ask to know
> What I was walling in or walling out,
> And to whom I was like to give offense.
> Something there is that doesn't love a wall,
> That wants it down. I could say "Elves" to him,
> But it's not elves exactly, and I'd rather
> He said it for himself.

Then he goes on with the tragedy of the refusal to hear the call. Frost concludes the poem with these frightening words:

> He moves in darkness, as it seems to me,
> Not of woods only and the shade of trees,
> He will not go behind his father's saying.
> And he likes having thought of it so well
> He says again, "Good fences make good
>   neighbours." *(Henry Holt, 1930)*

What particularly intrigues me about the poem are the two words: *spring* and *elves*. "Spring is the mischief in me." That spring is alive in the church. The creative, passionate efforts at all levels to renew and refill the church are a part of that spring. "Something there is that doesn't love a wall," and we've got to get in touch with that something. What continues to tear the walls down? What is it? "I could say elves to him but it's not elves exactly." What is it then? What is it that sends the frozen ground swells under? What exactly, if it isn't elves? "I'd rather he said it for himself."

Another poem that demonstrates the call to adventure is a short but powerful piece by the German poet, Rainer Maria Rilke.

Sometimes a man stands up during supper
and walks outdoors, and keeps on walking,
because of a church that stands somewhere in the East.

And his children say blessings on him as if he were
dead.

And another man, who remains inside his house,
stays there, inside the dishes and in the glasses,
so that his children have to go far out into the world
toward that same church which he forgot.

(Harper and Rowe, 1981)

"Sometimes a man stands up during supper," going about the ordinary course of events in his life. He decides to go out walking, and he keeps on walking . . . the journey. "Because of a church that stands somewhere in the East." Why the East? Is it a metaphor for the new day? A metaphor for dawn? A metaphor of freshness? It stands somewhere that he can't identify, but whatever the price, he's going to go looking for it. His children come to revere him as one who is dead.

I've thought often about the meaning of this poem. I believe it refers to a man who lives outside the bounds of his ordinary daily life. He sets an example for his children and his spouse. He lives with purpose more meaningful than merely his work, and people don't have to wait until the man dies to pay homage to his courage. "Blessed are those who hunger and thirst for righteousness, for they shall be filled." *(Matthew 5:6)*

But the other man remained inside his own house, inside his own patterns of thinking...inside the old ways of doing things. He stays there even "inside the dishes and in the glasses"! He's simply imprisoned in the mundane of his constant surroundings. Let's turn on the TV again and get lost, so we don't have to think. Let's stay busy. Let's just stay in the glasses, in the alcohol, in the routine, whatever it is. His children must go far out into the world toward that same church which he forgot.

I hear this as a commentary about some churches which people today are leaving behind. Those churches are also stuck "inside the dishes and in the glasses." Their children will hear a call to adventure and will now go far out in search of the values and spiritual significance they need. In many cases they have forgotten all about the church of their fathers, and that church has forgotten them.

Edgar Lee Masters wrote about the refusal to accept the call in a poem entitled "George Grey." Masters, in the *Spoon River Anthology*, regularly visited a cemetery in his town to study the tombstones of the various people buried there. As he spent time in that cemetery, he imagined how these people might have lived, and so was led to write poetry as if the dead persons were speaking in his mind. One such person was George Grey. In the following poem George Grey speaks from his grave:

> *I have studied many times*
> *The marble which was chiseled for me*
> *A boat with a furrowed sail that rests in the harbor.*
> *In truth it pictures not my destination*
> *But my life.*
> *For love was offered me and I shrank from its*
> *   disillusionment.*
> *Sorrow knocked on the door but I was afraid.*
> *Ambition called to me but I dreaded the chances.*
> *Yet all the while I hungered for meaning in my life.*
>
> *And now I know, that we must lift the sail*

And catch the winds of destiny
Wherever they drive the boat.
To put meaning in one's life may end in madness,
But life without meaning, is the torture
Of restlessness and vague desire
It is a boat longing for the sea and yet afraid.

(Signet Classic, 1992)

Compare this to the parable of the talents from scripture, when Jesus admonishes the small-mindedness of the one-talent servant who was not about to let that talent go. The man knew the master was harsh, and he wasn't going to pay the consequences connected with taking a chance. *(Matthew 25:14-30)*

If one responds to the call, there is most certainly an immediate struggle with resistance and it often shows up in the form of people on the outside. In Luther's time it was the Inquisition. In Christ's time it was the Sanhedrin. In Martin Luther King Jr.'s time, it was the racist in the south and the bigot in the north. Resistance in one form or another, the fear of letting go of the old, must always be overcome.

When resistance is engaged, the journey is changed in an unusual way: one encounters a mysterious appearance of help. I've seen this happen many times in my own life and countless times in the lives of others. Oriental philosophers say that when the student is ready, the teacher will appear. It's a strange phenomenon described by Carl Jung as synchronicity.

Ignatious of Loyola referred to it as confirmation, a pattern of coincidences confirming the chosen path. These coincidences begin to happen when one's mind is set to following a spiritual path, to living in truth. When one sets her or his mind to being real, to discovering an authentic identity for oneself, and to knowing where God's presence intersects the chosen path, nature applauds and manna is sent from heaven. The right book comes, the right article comes, a person knocks on your door...it's unexplainable, and yet it happens all the time. It's what Jesus referred to as our daily bread.

The nourishment is given to overcome the resistance and to help us "cross the threshold". Now the thesis is nailed to the wall. Now you apply for college or the job. Now you get the lawyer. You do something, you act. You cross the threshold, and when that threshold is crossed, you'll never be the same again.

When a person crosses that threshold, there is sometimes the feeling of violating sacred patterns and old traditions. It was at this point that Luther counseled people to "sin bravely," because the only way out of the hell is to act against the gods who are not really gods. The gods who are simply trying to preserve the status quo for their own invested reasons must be toppled. Naturally, as anyone performs this heroic act, he or she will be nervous and scared, and may even feel guilty. By speaking the truth and risking the wrath of those whom Campbell calls "the guardians of the gate," those who would hold on to the old form at all costs, one has indeed crossed the threshold. The die is cast. There is no turning back.

Initiation—Illumination

The second phase of the journey is called initiation, which basically involves a set of trials, often culminating in defeat. Along the road of travail there is ultimately an encounter with despair.

When I first began dealing with despair in my business, my wife became very uneasy. Also acting as my coach, she has encouraged me as a male to get in touch with my own emotions and to express them. One day, trying desperately to understand what I was feeling, I realized, "What I'm feeling is despair." She said, "Oh, my gosh, that's scary." I told her I knew that...I was scared too, but it was what I was really feeling. What I now know is that, just as an alcoholic must hit bottom, so must we also go through despair. This is part of the growth process. This is part of the disillusionment of Good Friday and Holy Saturday.

Herman Hesse in his book *Journey to the East* said, "Despair is the result of each earnest attempt to go through life with virtue, justice and understanding and to fulfill the requirements. Children live on one side of despair, the awakened on the other side." *(Peter Owen: 1972)*

I worked one time with a group of supervisors in an organization, all of whom were really "down." The room was so full of dark energy that I finally had to stop the process and get a better understanding of what was taking place. "Hey look," I said, "We're not getting anywhere. We've got to figure out what's going on here. Let's go around the room and have each one of you tell us what you're feeling."

The first person said, "Well, I'm feeling discouraged." The second person said, "I'm feeling down." The third person said, "I'm feeling depressed." The fourth person said, "I'm feeling despair."

The fifth person said, "No you're not." I stopped and said, "What did you say?" The man just went blank; he was in denial.

So I returned to the fourth person, and asked him to repeat what he had said. "I said I was in despair." I addressed the fifth person again, "How does that make you feel?"

And he said, "Oh man, it's okay to be down; it's okay to be discouraged; it's okay even to be depressed, but despair, that sounds like death."

And I said, "Right, something is dying. We need to discover what it is, acknowledge it, and then let it go."

If we are to be the church in a changing world, then the question we must ask ourselves is, "What is dying? What's dying in the world? What's dying in the church?" Then we must take the heroic journey and ask ourselves, what is dying inside of us?

"Unless a grain of wheat falls into the earth and dies, it remains just a single grain; but if it dies, it bears much fruit."*(John 12:24)* "For those who want to save their life will lose it, and those who lose their life for my sake, and for the sake of the gospel, will save it."*(Mark 8:35)*

"The theologians of the future must be a generation looking for a new language to restate the ancient truth."

Every person is called to walk through death many times. The call is to acknowledge death, to acknowledge the liturgies that aren't working, the forms, the rituals that aren't working, the belief codes that aren't working.

Thirty years ago in Austria, I heard Karl Rahner predict, *"the theologians of the future must be a generation looking for a new language in which to restate the ancient truth."*

Robert Frost wrote a poem about despair entitled Acquainted With The Night.*(Henry Holt, 1969)* It describes that state in the journey during which everything is numb, "when time is neither wrong or right." All meaning has been drained from function and forms, and life simply doesn't matter. One could easily lie down and die.

My mother went through surgery many years ago. As we stayed with her in the hospital, days just seemed to go on in pain and discomfort. Once she looked at me and asked, "What time is it?" I didn't have my watch on, and I said without thinking, "the time is neither wrong or right." It didn't make any difference what time it was. It could have been 4 o'clock in the morning; it could have been 4 o'clock in the afternoon . . . it just didn't make any difference. And that's all right. That stage of the journey, the time of despair, has to be validated in us. Death is a fact of life.

I believe one of the practical heresies in Christianity is the tendency to, at all cost, avoid the pain of death... to stay away from the Good Fridays. That is not what the gospel message is all about. The message is not that we won't have to descend into hell, but that we will never have to descend into hell alone.

The joy of the Christian experience, according to Jesus, is the joy of the woman who has given birth after great suffering. It is the joy of release from the effort, having raced the good race, fought the good fight. Yes, it is essential that the teaching be always the same: pick up your cross daily and follow me. There is no easy way. The only way out is through.

The way of the cross is hard. It calls for yielding ego to be crushed or ridiculed time and again, until down on our knees, we finally say, Lord, have mercy. This is the heroic journey. It's the journey Christ exemplified and the way we are called to follow. It is the road less travelled. "Enter through the narrow gate. For wide is the gate and broad is the road that leads to destruction, and many enter through it. But small is the gate and narrow the road that leads to life, and only a few find it." *(Matthew 7:13,4)*

What is the reward for seeing this journey through to the end? "Initiation" is indeed the proper terminology here, for we are initiated into the spiritual life, as our egos, our selfishness, our habits, greed, avarice, materialism, or whatever else gets burned away in the suffering of life. Like gold, we are purified in the crucible. In the process, something happens very deep within our souls, when this deep reservoir of divine energy, the Holy Spirit, begins to make its presence known. The Spirit of a living God begins to illumine, console, purify, and guide us. This period of illumination and deeper understanding just blows in like the wind. It just happens, or as the maxim states: "Invited or not, God will be present." The wind blows, and one is suddenly illuminated. Understanding comes in the form of a quiet, calm sense of direction, and there is no question but that God is present.

We have all had this experience at one time or another. It may have been while sitting quietly spellbound by nature, while making love, or when looking into the face of one's baby. At that moment everything is right. Everything fits.

One of my friends was running one day out at White Water State Park, when he had the experience of being outside of his body. In this state he just knew everything fit together. When he returned from the run, he was a changed person. It was an experience of propriety, that things were properly placed. His life was in order. Such must have been the experience of E.E. Cummings as described in the following poem.

i thank You God for most this amazing
day: for the leaping greenly spirits of trees
and a blue true dream of sky; and for everything
which is natural which is infinite which is yes

(i who have died am alive again today,
and this is the sun's birthday; this is the birth
day of life and of love and wings: and of the gay
great happening illimitably earth)

how should tasting touching hearing seeing
breathing any—lifted from the no
of all nothing—human merely being
doubt unimaginable You?

(now the ears of my ears awake and
now the eyes of my eyes are opened)
    e.e. cummings *(Harcourt, Brace &Co.:1926)*

"Now the ears of my ears awake and now the eyes of my eyes are opened" — a transformation that reminds us of what

Jesus said, let those who have eyes to see, see, and those who have ears to hear, hear. (Matthew 13:15-17) That hearing and seeing comes about through the internal crucifixion of one's own selfishness, of one's own baseness, of one's own trepidation, until we finally surrender and allow God's spirit into our lives.

Edna St. Vincent Millay wrote a poem at the age of nineteen that describes once more this initiation experience. In "Renascence" she is taking in the incomparable beauty of the world, when she has a mystical death experience. Imagining herself as dead and buried six feet underground, she, having taken on all the sins of the world, is suddenly illuminated by the tomb bursting open.

> Ah! Up then from the ground sprang I
> And hailed the earth with such a cry
> As is not heard save from a man
> Who has been dead and lives again...
> ...O God, I cried, no dark disguise
> Can e'er hereafter hide from me
> Thy radiant identity!
> Thou canst not move across the grass
> But my quick eyes will see Thee pass,
> Nor speak, however silently,
> But my hushed voice will answer Thee.
> I know the path that tells Thy way
> Through the cool eve of every day;
> God, I can push the grass apart
> And lay my finger on Thy heart!

The poem closes with these words:

> The world stands out on either side
> No wider than the heart is wide;

Above the world is stretched the sky,
No higher than the soul is high.
The heart can push the sea and land
Farther away on either hand;
The soul can split the sky in two,
And let the face of God shine through.
But East and West will pinch the heart
That can not keep them pushed apart;
And he whose soul is flat the sky
Will cave in on him by and by. (Harper & Rowe: 1917)

The Return

You've made the decision to break loose from the old, been directionless in the desert for what seemed like forever, and finally received a new wisdom. Now, armed with this boon for the future, your challenge is to organize your life around this new understanding. This last stage is the return to the world following an inner experience, the trip down from mountain top illumination. One must carry this new consciousness back to one's daily life.

The change of the church or the change of the world is essentially an internal, one-by-one, mind change. It is more than changing programs or liturgy; it's changing consciousness. So, when your consciousness is transformed, and you return to a world of people who have not yet had the experience, inevitably the message you carry back sounds somewhat crazy. It's not surprising that Jesus was crucified.

Remember, there are two reasons
the journey is heroic: the first is
the separation; the second is the return.

Throughout history the prophets and the artists have always been criticized because their illuminations from the mountain top or the silence of their own souls didn't make sense to those who hadn't experienced the vision. When a Martin Luther King, Jr. comes along, or Ghandi comes into the world, it seems inevitable they will be killed. It is inevitable that they will be silenced because they don't fit the forms and structures protected by the guardians of the gate.

The return is hard work. You may be told that you're a heretic or you may be told you've lost your sanity or your faith, but you need to summon that same source of courage you used to begin your journey. Remember, there are two reasons the journey is heroic: The first is the separation; the second is the return.

Joseph Campbell says it like this, "...we have not even to risk the adventure alone, for the heroes of all time have gone before us. The labyrinth is thoroughly known. We have only to follow the thread of the hero's path, and where we had thought to find an abomination, we shall find a god. And where we had thought to slay another, we shall slay ourselves. Where we had thought to travel outward, we will come to the center of our own existence. And where we had thought to be alone, we will be with all the world." *(Doubleday: 1988)*

Yes, that's the way it is. Where we had thought to find an abomination (things we do according to the old forms—new paradigms that butt up against the old in an abominable way) we find God at the end of the path. And where we looked outside for the problem and had thought to slay another, we shall end up slaying ourselves. And where we had thought to travel outward, we find the kingdom is, as always, within. The kingdom is the silence of our own hearts. There, where we had thought to be alone, we shall be with all the world.

That is the journey of change. It is the journey to which we all are called, if we listen to the stirrings of our souls.

As we follow those stirrings, we will encounter resistance, but then, inexplicably, but with absolute certainty, we will receive the manna that we need for today. We will be fed the article or the person or the book that we need to inspire us to take one more step on the path. And we'll cross thresholds that make us feel evil or foolish, and we may be frightened or confused by the strength of the opposition. In the process at some point, we will be confronted by death, the letting go of the old things that smell now of death, and we will get through that valley. By staying just a little longer in the void, the Spirit will inevitably speak. In the silence God will speak. God will illumine, console, and inspire us, and will point the path and provide the resources we need. Of this you may be assured.

I hope I have encouraged you in your efforts to embody God's presence in a desperate world. We serve not only by our strength, but also through our vulnerability and woundedness. We must learn to embrace the cross, the deaths, and resurrections along the way. Dying is a way of life. So is being reborn.

"Very truly, I tell you, unless a grain of wheat falls into the earth and dies, it remains just a single grain; but if it dies, it bears much fruit." (John 12:24)

Acknowledgements

I wish to express my appreciation to the people at Prince of Peace Publishing whose encouragement and support helped me to give voice, first at the Changing Church Conferences and now in this book. I am especially grateful to Pastors Merv Thompson and Hal Olson, but most especially to Gail Steel, whose patience, persistence and strength carried the manuscript to its completion.

I have been blessed with many teachers in my life: my parents, sisters and brother first, my wife's parents and siblings, then a series of outstanding instructors and mentors, most notably Bernard Cooke, George Klubertanz, and Karl Rahner. As is apparent from the text, I have been profoundly influenced by Rollo May, Carl Jung, Joseph Campbell, and M. Scott Peck. To these and many others who have helped shape my thinking, I am profoundly grateful.

Ignatius of Loyola, through his Spiritual Exercises, led me to what he called "the intimate knowledge" of the person of Jesus of Nazareth. His parables and other teachings remain for me the clearest, simplest and most profound psychological truths I have discovered.

My greatest teacher has been my wife and business partner, Mary Mead Lofy. She and our children, John, Ann-Marie, and Bill, have taught me beyond measure the transformative possibilities inherent in the safe environment of forgiveness and unfailing devotion and love. So have my friends Han and Nelson van den Blink, Bill Olszewski, Diane and Bill Manahan, Bev and Steve Palmquist, Lori and Dave Ruthenbeck.

This book flows from a fountain of deep gratitude to these and others too numerous to mention: friends, clients and students alike. If at times my words sing, it is because of them; the shortcomings of the book are my own.

Footnotes

The Heroic Journey

Campbell, Joseph, *Hero With A Thousand Faces*. (Princeton, NJ: Princeton University Press, 1968).

Eliot, T.S., 1909-1935, *Collected Poems*. (Orlando, FL: Harcourt Brace & Co., 1932).

Garrow, David, *Bearing the Cross*. (New York: Morrow, 1986).

Jung, Carl G., *The Collected Works of C.G. Jung* Princeton University Press (Bollingen Series XX); London: Routledge & Kegan Paul; Vol. 5. *Symbols of Transformation*. 1956.

A Passion for Form

Alsop, Stuart, *Stay of Execution*. (Philadelphia, PA: Lippincott,1973).

Barker, Joel, *Discovering the Future 1st ed*. (Lake Elmo, MN: ILI Press, 1985).

May, Rollo, *The Courage to Create*. (New York: Norton, 1975).

Minuchin, Salvador, *Families and Family Therapy*. (Cambridge, MA.: Harvard University Press, 1974).

Sheehy, Gail, *Passages: Predictable Crises of Adult Life*. (New York: Dutton, 1976).

The Dance of Spirit

May, Rollo, *The Courage to Create*. (New York: Norton, 1975).

Peck, Scott Morgan, *The Different Drum: Community-making and Peace*. (New York: Simon and Schuster, 1987).

Spirit in Form

Bridges, William, *Transitions*. (Reading, PA: Addison-Wesley, 1980).

Lindbergh, Anne Morrow, *A Gift From the Sea* (New York: Vintage Books, 1959).

Transformation of Consciousness

Cummings, E.E.. *Poems 1923-1954* (Orlando: Harcourt Brace, 1926).

Consciousness Precedes Being

Campbell, Joseph, 1904-1987, *Power of Myth 1st ed., with Bill Moyers.* (New York: Doubleday Bell Publishing Group, 1988).

"The Revolution Has Just Begun," *Time* March 5, 1990. (Time, Inc.).

Three Basic Principles

Kierkegaard, Soren, *A Kierkegaard Anthology,* ed. Robert Bretall. (Princeton: Princeton U.P., 1946).

The Three Phases

Campbell, Joseph, Hero With A Thousand Faces. (Princeton, NJ: Princeton University Press, 1968).

Cummings, E.E., *Poems 1923-1954* (Harcourt Brace & Co.: 1926).

Frost, Robert, "Acquainted With the Night," *The Poetry of Robert Frost,* edited by Edward Connery Lathem. (New York: Henry Holt & Co. Inc., 1969).

Frost, Robert, "Mending Wall" (New York: Henry Holt & Co., Inc., 1930).

Hesse, Herman, *Journey to the East.* (Chester Springs: Peter Owen, 1972).

Masters, Edgar Lee, *Spoon River Anthology.* (New York: Signet Classic, 1992).

Millay, Edna St. Vincent, "Renascence" *The Collected Poems of Edna St. Vincent Millay.* (New York: Harper & Row Publishers Inc., 1917).

Rilke, Rainer Maria, *Selected Poems of Rainer Maria Rilke.* edited by Robert Bly (New York: Harper & Row, 1981).